THE EVERYDAY
PROJECT MANAGER

THE EVERYDAY PROJECT MANAGER

A Primer for Learning the Principles of Successful Project Management

BY JEREMY NICHOLLS

A PRODUCTIVITY PRESS BOOK

First published 2021
by Routledge
600 Broken Sounds Parkway #300, Boca Raton FL, 33487

and by Routledge
2 Park Square, Milton Park, Abingdon, Oxon, OX14 4RN

Routledge is an imprint of the Taylor & Francis Group, an informa business

© 2021 Taylor & Francis

The right of Jeremy Nicholls to be identified as the author of this work has been asserted by him in accordance with sections 77 and 78 of the Copyright, Designs and Patents Act 1988.

ISBN: 978-0-367-55133-9 (hbk)
ISBN: 978-0-367-41678-2 (pbk)
ISBN: 978-0-367-81738-1 (ebk)

Typeset in Minion Pro
by Deanta Global Publishing Services, Chennai, India

Contents

PHASE 2   Design and Planning

PHASE 3   Build and Execute

PHASE 4   Project Closure and Lessons Learned

Acknowledgments

As I sat down to write a book on the underlying principles of project management, I did so out of a need to get my own thoughts down on paper as much as anything. While I hoped that the information contained in this book might be helpful to others, it was beyond my wildest dreams to think I might actually see this in print.

Like any project manager though, I must acknowledge that this would be simply impossible without the considerable efforts of others.

I am indebted for so much of the good advice contained in this volume first and foremost to my original mentor – James Mace. James was the first person to teach me about the relationship between vision, benefits, and objectives and much, much more besides, though he can be found these days sailing around the world. Wherever you are James, fair winds.

My project management career has been shaped in huge degrees first by Tim Bretman and, more recently, Danny Hargest. For the countless opportunities you have given me (both for success and learning), I am forever grateful. Jo Horton, Andy Clarke, and the rest of the team at CCM have also taught me a great deal and I hope they will recognize many of our shared experiences within these pages.

For helping me realize my desire to turn this from pet project into the actual, published book you hold in your hands, my sincere thanks go to Rowland Hayler – who proves the point made on a few occasions in this book, that the value of a cup of coffee with a colleague really cannot be underestimated! Thank you for your support and for introducing me to Jeanne Levine. Jeanne, thank you for all those late night (in London)/late afternoon (in New Jersey) phone calls as I worked through early drafts and you worked to connect me with a publisher.

Huge thanks go to my sister-from-another-mister, Genevieve Binefa, who read an early draft and provided feedback which immeasurably improved the content. Thank you, Free.

Where I have failed to properly impart the lessons that have been taught to me over the years, or correctly adopt the feedback and guidance I've received, the failure is mine entirely. I do hope those who have been so generous with their time, mentorship, support, and guidance will forgive such errors.

And finally, it is perhaps unsurprising that I wish to thank my family. The love and support I have enjoyed throughout my career in project management are indescribable and unsurpassable. Thank you to Mum, Dad, and Ashley for the early years and to Louise, Madeleine, and Harrison for putting up with me more recently. You are incomparably, wonderfully supportive people and I cannot tell you how grateful I am for that.

But most of all to Louise. Really, it's you.

About the Author

Jeremy Nicholls found project management after trying his hand at several other careers. It remains the single best career he's ever stumbled into accidentally.

He has delivered projects in several sectors covering several disciplines. He's been an IT project manager in the finance profession; a construction project manager in the aviation profession; and a business change project manager in the legal profession. He rather hopes that this justifies his belief that project management is a skill that transcends the area in which it is delivered.

He has delivered software projects, new ways of working, physical buildings, and advice on project management best practice to a number of household-name clients over the course of more than a decade.

In his spare time, he plays jazz piano and enjoys nothing more than an evening spent watching a movie with his two children before cooking a meal with his wife.

Introduction Part One

WHAT IS THE EVERYDAY PROJECT MANAGER?

We live in a world of projects. From complex, national infrastructure projects to the small, personal projects we each undertake, wherever there is a group of activities, a budget, and a target date, there is a project.

Success in business is almost wholly reliant on an ability to implement change effectively – be it a computer system upgrade that gives you the edge on your competitor, bringing a new product to market, adopting new ways of working, or completely redefining the approach your company takes. Success and survival in business rely on change and the way that business implements change is through projects. Therefore, if you work in the world of business, sooner or later the chances are that you will be involved in a project, as a stakeholder, advisor, Sponsor or possibly running it – that is, as the project manager.

Business notwithstanding, all of us at one time or another need to deliver a project. It might be building a garden shed, putting on a show or event, moving house, preparing for a wedding, or any of the numerous things in life that require a bit of thought and preparation. And all of these things become less stressful with even the most basic understanding of how to deliver projects. You don't need to be a famous chef in order to bake a cake, but having an understanding of the basics of cookery will help you get a better result each time. You don't need to be an accountant to manage the family budget, but knowing how to use a spreadsheet will make it considerably easier.

And so it follows that you don't need to be a professional project manager to benefit from an understanding of what makes projects tick and apply them to the projects in your life.

Welcome to the world of *The Everyday Project Manager.*

WHO IS THIS BOOK FOR?

Anyone. Anyone at all who needs or wants to deliver a project – and sooner or later, that's everyone. Specifically though, this book is aimed at the following people:

- **Project leaders and any member of a project team.** If you have been assigned to work on a project team – maybe you're even sponsoring or leading a project – then reading this book will help you to relate to others on your team. By following the principles laid out in this book, and understanding who does what (and who *should* be doing what), the whole team will work more effectively to deliver the desired goal.
- **The beginner project manager.** If you're just starting out on a career in project management, or you're considering it and would like to learn a bit more, this book will help you get your head around some of the key concepts within project management so you can get a feel for the subject.
- **The seasoned project manager.** It might be that you have been delivering projects for years, but the best project managers take time out occasionally to remind themselves of the basics. This book is intended to give an overview of project management, so acts well as a high-level refresher. You may even be at the point in your career where you are mentoring others – this book will be useful to structure and guide mentoring sessions.
- **The layperson.** If you are interested in understanding the basic principles of project management. Perhaps you've been given a project to deliver at work, or have a personal project such as planning a wedding or building an extension. You don't need to study for weeks or become a fully qualified project manager, but an understanding of the basics will definitely help you to reach your goal.
- **You.** Trust me, whoever you are, there will be something in the pages that follow that will help you in some way. The information in this book is derived from years of experience (both mine and others') that I have attempted to distill down to the essentials – the nuggets of gold in the enormous mine of project management. There will be something for everyone – the skills of project management are also excellent life skills and you will find yourself achieving more in life

and in work by following the principles, tools, and practices in this book.

THE EVERYDAY PROJECT MANAGER VS THE PROFESSIONAL PROJECT MANAGER

The skills and concepts detailed in the following pages are those that the average person can easily pick up and start putting to use. They are everyday (that is, commonplace) and should be simple to understand and implement. They are also the skills and the concepts that the best professional project managers use. Every. Day.

For example, understanding the difference between the benefits and the objectives of a project isn't something that is simply learnt at the start of your career and then consigned to the textbooks. It is an understanding that is vital to the delivery of every project at all times. Again: the best project managers use these skills **every single day**.

However, there is a cautionary note. In an attempt to distill the essence of the project management skill set and key concepts, some of the nuance and detail is necessarily lost. In this book, I have done so consciously. Much of the nuance is useful or of interest to project management professionals and experts only and is therefore not helpful in an introductory approach to the subject. That said, I will endeavor to point out where project management in the "professional world" may benefit from a more in-depth understanding of the subject.

For the most part though, we'll focus on the everyday skills that will enhance project delivery regardless of your level of experience.

THE STRUCTURE OF THIS BOOK

I have attempted to structure this book to follow the typical lifecycle of a project. Projects obviously vary wildly, but most (broadly) follow a pattern of Start-up ⇒ Design ⇒ Execute ⇒ Close, though there are many variations on this theme. Within each of these phases there are certain activities that you will need to undertake and so I have divided the book according to the phases, with each chapter focusing on an area or activity that needs to be undertaken during that phase. Not everyone joins a project at the start (in fact, few do), so it is hoped that this structure will allow the reader to dip in and out in order to cut straight to the activity they are currently involved in, interested in, or considering.

At the end of each chapter you will also find a summary of the key points to take away from the chapter. These summaries are themselves collated at the end of the book so that you can have a sort of project health checklist. By reviewing the "In Summary" section, you will hopefully be able to identify areas for improvement within your project or – better yet – satisfy yourself that everything that should be considered on a project has been.

WHAT THIS BOOK IS AND WHAT IT ISN'T

Finally, this book is not intended as an exhaustive explanation of project management. It is not a "bible" containing everything you will ever need to know about project delivery.

Nor is it a manual that gives step-by-step information to deliver a perfect project every time. This book will not guarantee project success. Believe me, if such a book existed I would either be incredibly rich or out of a job!

What you will find is sufficient information to gain a broad understanding of the basics, alongside lots of ideas to improve projects, reduce stress, and manage everything else along the way.

I've endeavored to ensure each section is concise, with no lengthy explanations – I'll leave that to the more detailed project management manuals, of which there are plenty. In this book, I've tried to keep the information short but sweet, making it perfect for dipping into – either to learn about a specific element of project management or as a quick refresher.

Above all, it will give you the tools you need to immediately start delivering better projects and, in doing so, put more change into the world and get more out of life.

Introduction Part Two

SOME PROJECT MANAGEMENT DEFINITIONS

For this book, we are looking at The Everyday Project Manager – a person tasked with a single project to deliver and looking to understand the principles and techniques of project management to enable them to deliver successfully.

If you are currently working in an environment that delivers projects, you might be familiar with some terms which are useful to understand, as they provide a context for project delivery in general, but which will not be covered in detail in this book as they do not fit with The Everyday Project Manager remit described above.

However, because they are useful concepts to understand, and for completeness, I will briefly outline some definitions below along with some explanation (which will hopefully become obvious) as to why they are not covered in more detail in this book.

PROJECTS, PROGRAMS, AND PORTFOLIOS

It is worth distinguishing between projects, programs, and portfolios. The distinction has to do with the number of projects and their relation to one another. A project is a single, cohesive set of tasks that delivers an end result. It will produce a deliverable, or set of deliverables, so projects are said to create *outputs*.

A program is a group of projects which taken together deliver an *outcome*. In other words, it is a group of projects, all of which will deliver their outputs, but when all of these outputs are taken together, a broader outcome will be achieved. For example, let's imagine an organization wants to encourage more remote working. It identifies five pieces of work that could be undertaken to promote remote working and agrees to pursue three of them as projects. The three projects are: a software project which will roll out teleconferencing software to make it easier for remote workers to dial into meetings and follow presentations at home; a hardware rollout project to provide any identified remote workers with a laptop and mobile phone; and a Human Resources project to identify candidates for remote working and work with them to create new contracts and benefits packages accordingly. It could be argued that none of those projects on its own would deliver the organizational outcome of a workforce for whom remote working is a realistic option with, say, 25% of employees working remotely at least once a week. But taken together, those three projects will deliver outputs that make the outcome possible. Similarly, there might be no realistic justification to undertake just one of those projects without the others also being undertaken. The projects do not have merit in isolation. But taken together – as a program – the projects become justified as part of a larger initiative. A program, therefore, is a group of related projects whose outputs, together, deliver an outcome. A program will normally be run by a Program Manager who will have the project managers of each of the underlying projects as their direct reports.

Finally, a portfolio is the entire suite of projects and programs being undertaken by an organization, be it a department, business unit, or company as a whole. The portfolio may be made up of multiple individual, unrelated projects without any of them grouped as programs. It may be a series of programs all delivering their specific business outcomes with no standalone projects. Or it may (more usually) be a combination of programs and projects, all of which are delivering for the business. A portfolio is typically run by a Portfolio Manager who will have the project and program managers delivering within their portfolio as their direct reports (Figure 0.1).

Program and Portfolio Management are fascinating and exciting disciplines in their own right, but they are quite distinct from Project Management which is the focus of this book.

WATERFALL VS AGILE PROJECT MANAGEMENT

A word at this point on waterfall vs agile project management. You may have heard of these terms, you may not – it doesn't really matter. All you need to know is that they are different models for delivering projects.

```
PORTFOLIO

    PROGRAMME 1              PROGRAMME 2

      PROJECT 1                PROJECT 6

      PROJECT 2                PROJECT 7

      PROJECT 3
                               PROJECT 8
      PROJECT 4
                               PROJECT 9
      PROJECT 5
                               PROJECT 10
```

FIGURE 0.1
Projects, Programs, and Portfolios.

Waterfall is seen as the "traditional" way of delivering projects and takes its name from the way one task flows into another like a waterfall – especially when represented in a type of project plan known as a Gantt chart (Figure 0.2).

This style of project management works particularly well when the end-state is known or (relatively) easy to define. It is therefore favored in the world of, for example, construction, or engineering. It is seen as "traditional" project management, and most of the concepts discussed in this book are born from this model. As the tried-and-tested form of

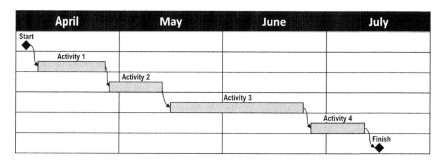

FIGURE 0.2
A Waterfall "Gantt" chart.

project management, it is the one that I recommend for The Everyday Project Manager. But that is not to say you shouldn't be aware of – or even actively seeking out – other models.

Agile project management is a more recent addition to the landscape. Used primarily in software development, it uses cycles of activity to gradually refine a solution (as opposed to working towards a pre-established solution). Agile is used when – at the outset of the project – you might not have a clear idea of the final state. It is effective for turning a *concept* into a reality, especially in a fast-moving environment (such as technology) where if you spend too long defining a solution, the world moves on. Each cycle of activity is known as a sprint and in each sprint you develop the solution a little further. A given sprint might introduce a new feature or work on a specific element of the project, but it allows you to evolve the solution over multiple iterations.

When considering the everyday projects that many of us will come into contact with, the vast majority are likely to follow a waterfall methodology. This is partly because waterfall is "traditional" project management – it has been around longer and is more firmly established in organizations. It is also better suited to projects where the end goal is reasonably well-defined. This book is for those people undertaking a project where they have a fairly clear idea of what they want to achieve. The information and techniques described in this book will help in *any* project – regardless of methodology – but are founded on waterfall principles. This is not to say the agile methodology is without merit. Far from it – and if you are interested in agile, I recommend you seek out other books on the subject. I hope and expect though (and years of experience tell me) that you will find your everyday projects are well suited to this form of delivery. As I say, *any* project can be delivered successfully using the approaches outlined in this book. So, without further ado, let's get started.

Phase 1

Project Start-Up

1

What Are We Doing Here?: The Vision, Benefits, and Objectives

If you want to build a ship, don't drum up the men to gather wood, divide the work and give orders. Instead, teach them to yearn for the vast and endless sea.

Antoine de Saint-Exupéry

IS THIS A PROJECT I SEE BEFORE ME?

It may seem to be stating the obvious, but to get the most from project management, you need a project.

Properties of projects include:

- A clear end-state that is different from the starting position.
- A beginning and (target) end date.
- An over-arching goal with several/numerous discrete tasks needed to deliver it.
- Multiple people or parties involved.

Things that are not projects:

- Maintenance work (e.g. gardening).
- Recurring tasks (e.g. weekly sports practice).

- Normal manufacturing processes or day-to-day business operations (e.g. car production).
- Ad hoc individual activities (e.g. cooking dinner).

For instance, gardening is not a project, but landscaping is. Keeping fit is not a project, but completing a marathon is. Cooking dinner is not a project, but organizing a dinner-dance is. The assembly of cars on a production line is not a project, but a team of people restoring a car is. Sometimes it's a subtle difference. Everything that follows is best applied to things that have the properties of a project.

WHERE TO BEGIN

Whether you are starting a new project, or taking over the reins of one that has been running for a while, you always need a starting point. For every project you undertake you should start with one simple question:

- What is it that we are trying to do?

Believe it or not, this question is often harder to answer than it may appear. I've taken over projects that have been running for several months where there are either multiple answers to that question or, worse yet, no answer at all. The simplest key to a project's success – and therefore the very quickest way to take a project and get it under your control – is to ensure there is a single, simple answer to that question and that the answer is shared and understood by everyone working on the project.

There are, however, three elements that go toward answering that question and it is no understatement to say: if you take nothing else from this book, understanding and agreeing the vision, benefits, and objectives of a project are the key to its success. It is as simple as that. And, of course, it's a lot more complicated.

DO YOU KNOW WHERE YOU'RE GOING?

The best organizations, and even the best departments within organizations, have a roadmap: a clear vision of where they would like to be and the means by which they will get there. This roadmap drives the everyday activity of the company as well as any changes it makes both internally and externally. And it is what drives projects.

In much the same way, at a personal level, you will have a vision of the person you want to be. This vision will inform the life goals – both short- and long-term – that you wish to achieve, which in turn inform the challenges and activities you undertake to get there.

These roadmaps – be they corporate or personal – are made up of three elements that are intrinsically linked and bound to one another, whilst remaining distinct from one another. In the world of project management, they are defined as the Vision, the Benefits, and the Objectives.

THE CASCADE

The three concepts of vision, benefits, and objectives can be thought of as having a cascading relationship. The vision provides the context for the benefits which in turn create the need for the objectives. It is a good test of how well-defined a project is to see if the project objectives (which define what the project will deliver) tie neatly back to the benefits (which define why you're delivering it) which in turn tie neatly back to the vision.

I cannot sufficiently emphasize how important it is to understand the difference between benefits and objectives, as they underpin every project, and poorly defined – or non-existent – benefits and objectives are a hallmark of project failure.

Let's have a look at each of these elements in a bit more detail (Figure 1.1)

THE VISION

The vision represents the over-arching context for the project – be that personal, departmental, organizational, local, national, or even global. So, a sustainability project could be framed within the context of the global need to fight climate change, for instance. At the other end of the scale, it might be very personal, for example: "to become happier in life, by pursuing the things that make me happy." The vision is non-specific – it

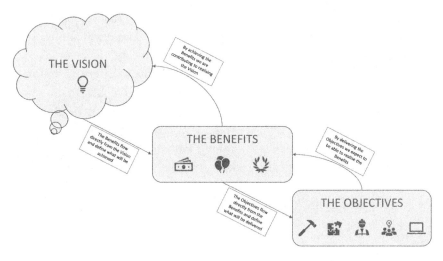

FIGURE 1.1
The vision, benefits, and objectives are inextricably linked to one another.

sets out the desired end-state, but does not specify how to get there. But it becomes the foundation stone upon which change is built. Once you identify and understand the type of change you want to create, you can begin to better identify the means of getting there, and package up work that will deliver that goal.

Examples of Vision Statements:

- To have a world-class project delivery organization.
- To increase the value of my house.
- To be the cleanest energy provider in the country.
- To offer outstanding customer service.
- To have a beautiful, memorable wedding day.

It is important to note that not all projects will have, or link back to, a vision. I mention the vision because it is an integral part of how a lot of projects come into being, even when the vision is not explicit. It can be useful though to understand the vision and maybe even to create it, in order to explain the wider context for undertaking the project. However, even the casual reader will appreciate it is possible to get on and do things without necessarily needing to set them within a wider context or strategy. Therefore, it is possible to have a project without an explicit vision. However, a project absolutely must have express benefits and objectives, as these will define the project and be the measure of its success. The vision gives birth to the project, which is made up of benefits and objectives.

BENEFITS: THE WHY

The benefits of a project describe why we are undertaking the work. They are the outcome(s) which should arise as a result of the project being delivered. As such, the benefits are owned by the customer (also known as the Sponsor – see Chapter 4) and it is the customer – **not the project manager**[*] – who is responsible for realizing them.[†]

Benefits should also be measurable; what's more, that measure should be outlined at the start of the project.

The list of benefits should not be too long. If there are more than three, it might be worth considering whether this is not one project but two. In practice, it is unlikely that a single project would deliver a great long list of benefits. That is not to say that the benefits will be small monetarily – in fact, they might amount to millions in revenue – but they should be few in number. In some cases, there will be just a single benefit.

To help frame the benefits when you are writing them, try writing them as statements beginning with the phrase "I want to see …."

On the next page are some examples of benefits and measures. As a bonus, I've also included the broader vision that might give rise to such a benefit (Table 1.1).

As you can see, the benefit and its associated measure are often two sides of the same coin, such that a benefit which states the intention is to achieve "A reduction in company operating costs" has the almost identical measure "Reduction in company operating costs of $30,000 a year." In any event, the measure should specify exactly how – in quantifiable terms – it will be demonstrated that the intended benefit has been achieved.

In summary, the benefits are what the Sponsor of the project wants to achieve as a result of the work. Typically, the benefits will accrue to the Sponsor – that is to say, it is the Sponsor who will actually *receive* the

---

[*] I've put this in bold. If I could, I'd put it in skywriting and burn it in ten-foot-high letters onto the side of a hill. This is important. The Sponsor owns the Benefits, the Project Manager owns the Objectives, and the two should never be confused.

[†] See Chapter 4 for things to consider when Sponsor and Project Manager are the same person (and they're both you!).

benefits once the project is complete. They commission the project in order to attain the benefits that they desire, and they own the responsibility for ensuring that the benefits are ultimately realized.

But the benefits are just outcomes. Something actually needs to be done in order to achieve them. The benefits tell us why we are doing the project, but it is the objectives that tell us what we are actually doing.

TABLE 1.1

Examples of benefits, linked to vision

Vision: To increase company efficiency year-on-year.	
Expected Benefit (I want to see…)	**Measure**
An increase in factory output.	Factory output increases by 15% vs. the previous year.
Vision: To create a better environment by increasing sustainability.	
Expected Benefit (I want to see…)	**Measure**
A reduction in the amount of recyclable waste going to landfill.	After five years, 70% of recyclable waste is being diverted from landfill (compared to current levels).
Vision: To get more enjoyment from our home and garden.[a]	
Expected Benefit (I want to see…)	**Measure**
An outdoor area where we enjoy spending time and entertaining.	The back garden is re-landscaped to include a barbecue area.

[a] Note that, unlike the previous two examples, this vision would almost certainly be implicit. Whilst corporate vision statements tend to be explicit and often published publicly, personal ones are more likely to be implicit and unwritten.

OBJECTIVES: THE WHAT

The objectives describe what will be done in order to achieve the benefits. They describe what it is that the project will do. Projects are delivery vehicles and as such should focus on delivery. The objectives should therefore describe clear, deliverable items. There should be an obvious, easy-to-agree point at which the objective is considered delivered. I often encourage people to think in terms of "What does 'finished' look like? At what point can I, as Project Manager, consider my job done and walk away?" By asking questions like this, you can quickly draw out the objectives from most customers. By asking the customer to consider a finished state as well, you are also encouraging them to think in terms of completed deliverables rather than open-ended pieces of work. Remember, a project is not open-ended, but a clearly defined set of finite, discrete objectives and associated activities. As such, objectives should be linked to *success criteria* – statements that describe what "finished" looks like, i.e. the agreed criteria by which we will judge the objective delivered.

And, importantly: **the project manager owns the Objectives.**[*][†]

The project manager is accountable for the delivery of the objectives and nothing more. The Sponsor, as the customer and ultimately, the receiver of the benefits, is accountable for the benefits. It is true that completion of the objectives should ultimately lead to the realization of the benefits (assuming care has been taken to ensure they are truly linked), but the project manager's job is complete when the objectives have been delivered.

This leads to an extremely counter-intuitive notion: the project can be completely successful without delivering any of the benefits. But if we step through just one of the previous examples, it should become clearer why that's the case.

WHY THE SPONSOR OWNS THE BENEFITS AND THE PROJECT MANAGER OWNS THE OBJECTIVES

Let's say I'm a factory manager and I want to increase the revenue generated by my factory (the Vision). There are several ways I could do this, but I decide that the one I want to pursue is increasing the productivity of the factory, and I set a target of a 15% increase in output (the Benefit). But I can't just *do* a 15% increase in output. I must do *something* to achieve it. So, I speak to consultants and colleagues (or maybe I just sit in a room on my own and think about the problem), and I arrive at the conclusion that the best way to do this would be to increase the number of product assembly stations. If I increase them, I increase productivity. Then I assign a member of my team as project manager and set them the objective of installing five additional stations and hiring five more people to work at them.

---

[*] I've put this in bold. If I could, I'd put it in skywriting and burn it in ten-foot-high letters onto the side of a hill. This is important. The Sponsor owns the Benefits, the Project Manager owns the Objectives, and the two should never be confused.

[†] Yes, I've deliberately repeated the footnote. It's **that** important.

Now, hopefully we can agree that, if the project manager installs the five stations and hires five additional people, she has done her job. Furthermore, it is not really her concern whether that results in a 15% productivity increase – that's my concern as Sponsor. Nor is it her fault if the expected 15% increase fails to materialize – she has delivered the project objectives.

Similarly, I have assigned a project manager to deliver the outputs that I believe will achieve my benefit. Therefore, I would be doubling-up if I too got involved in the delivery itself – that's why I hired a project manager. I expect them to keep me updated on progress and let me know of any potential issues along the way, but *they* are responsible for delivering the objectives – not me. I may be pursuing several such initiatives, each with their own set of benefits. It is not in my interests to get bogged down in the delivery, but I do want to make absolutely sure that the project managers deliver what they say they will, so I hold them accountable for the objectives.

Finally, the benefits are not typically realized the moment a project has finished. In some cases, it can take years for the benefits to be realized. For example, I might expect a 15% productivity increase *over the course of the following year*. Perhaps I want the assembly points installed and the technicians hired ahead of a six-month busy period. The project objectives have been delivered, but I won't see the full benefit until we're at the other end of the busy period, six months later. Am I going to keep the project manager involved for all that time? To what end? Their job is done, even if the benefit has not yet been delivered.

So, as you can see, it is vitally important to be clear on the benefits and objectives, as there are accountabilities associated with each one. They must be closely linked to one another, whilst also being separate in both nature and ownership.

To help frame the objectives when you are writing them, try writing them as statements beginning with the phrase "The Project will …."

Here are some examples of objectives and success criteria. As you will see, I have used the benefits from the previous example so you can see how they link and flow down to one another and all the way back to the vision (Table 1.2).

Remember: if you are not delivering the **objectives**, you are not delivering the **project**.

TABLE 1.2

Examples of objectives, linked to benefits

Vision: To increase company efficiency year-on-year.	
Expected Benefit	**Measure**
An increase in factory output.	Factory output increases by 15% vs. the previous year.
Objectives (The Project will…)	**Success Criteria**
Extend the production area to include five more stations for product assembly.	Additional five stations installed and ready to use.
Hire five more technicians to work on product assembly.	Total number of technicians increased by five people.
Vision: To create a better environment by increasing sustainability.	
Expected Benefit	**Measure**
A reduction in the amount of recyclable waste going to landfill.	After five years[a], 70% of recyclable waste is being diverted from landfill (compared to current levels).
Objectives (The Project will…)	**Success Criteria**
Provide recycling bins to all homes in the area.	One green and one blue recycling bin delivered to every house in the area.
Implement a new waste collection program to incorporate new recyclable waste collections.	Implementation of a new waste collection program for recyclable waste.
Communicate the changes to all households in the area.	Confirmation that a direct mailing has gone to each home in the area.
Vision: To get more enjoyment from our home and garden.	
Expected Benefit	**Measure**
An outdoor area where we enjoy spending time and entertaining.	The back garden is re-landscaped to include a barbecue area.
Objectives (The Project will…)	**Success Criteria**
Prepare the current area and undertake any enabling works.	Garden shed is removed and disposed of. Area is leveled and ready for decking.
Create a design for the outdoor area which includes decking, a built-in barbecue and outdoor lighting.	A completed design for the area is signed off by the customer.
Install decking & outdoor lighting.	Decking is completed in line with design. Outdoor lighting is installed and working.
Build a new barbecue area in the corner of the decked area.	Barbecue area is completed in line with design.

[a] Note the extended time period for benefits realization. Some projects (such as national, government-led infrastructure projects) might have decades before the full benefits case is expected to be realized.

Let me just say that again, because it's really important: *if you are not delivering the **objectives**, you are not delivering the **project**.* The objectives **are** the project, therefore work done on anything not relating to the project objectives is wasted. This can be counter-intuitive at times, particularly once the project is well underway. This is because the objectives can be well-established at the start of the project, but can easily be forgotten as the project gains momentum. People start working on all sorts of things that they *think* are part of the project (and might actually be worthy endeavors that deliver real benefit), but are *not* part of the originally agreed project.

For an example of how this happens, see the *Scope Creep* box in Chapter 3. For now though, to help avoid this, when delivering projects, it is worth starting each team meeting by going over the objectives. Yes, by several weeks in you will sound like a broken record (I've had audible groans when I've done this in project meetings), but you will ensure everyone is very clear on what needs to be done.

It is also useful to start each project by getting the whole team together and clearly stating what the project objectives are. This may seem obvious, but you would be amazed at how many projects start without a consensus on the objectives, or even a clear declaration of them. Once, when I was particularly keen to drive home the point, I put the project objectives up on the screen and read them out to the team. I then said,

> If you are not working on these objectives, that is fine, but then you are also not working on my project, so I will not be able to approve any time spent. Any work you do outside of these objectives, *even if it is adding value to the company as a whole,* is on your own time.

It was an extreme statement, and caused a few raised eyebrows, but it helped focus people's minds and got them to understand how important it is to remain focused on the objectives.

OBJECTIVES RELATING TO TIME, COST, OR QUALITY

It is worth noting that any objectives relating to time, cost, or quality (see Chapter 2: The Holy Trinity) are not really objectives. I have frequently seen objectives that state, for example, "the project must be delivered before the end of the Financial Year" or "the project must cost less than $250,000." It is always expected that the project will deliver on time, for the agreed-upon budget, and at the expected level of quality, so objectives relating to time, cost, and quality are implicit. Time, cost, and quality are all project *constraints*. They should be noted and clearly understood, but not treated as the purpose of the project.

LINKING THE CHAIN

As you can see from this chapter, there should be a clearly identifiable link that takes us from vision to benefit to objective and back again. This is really important. We do not want to be wasting our time working on something that does not achieve our goals, so by ensuring there is a strong link between benefits and objectives, we can be confident that any work done delivering the objectives stands a good chance of ultimately delivering the benefit and helping us to achieve our goals. Working back the other way, if you are the Sponsor and have a desired benefit that you want to achieve, you will want to be confident that the objectives, once delivered, set you up to get your benefit. And the same goes from benefit up to vision.

Because of the link between these, most projects could be summarized in the following format:

> As part of our **vision**, we want to achieve the **benefit**, so we are undertaking **project title**, which will **list objectives**.

Imagine, for example, a town council is undertaking a community recycling project. Their vision, benefits, and objectives might look much the same as the second example in the objectives section above and could be expressed as follows:

> In our manifesto, we pledged **to create a better environment by increasing sustainability (vision)**. As part of this pledge, we aim to achieve **a reduction in the amount of recyclable waste going to landfill (benefit)**, so we are undertaking the **Community Recycling Project (project title)**, through which we will **provide recycling bins to all homes in the area,**

implement a new waste collection program to incorporate new recyclable waste collections, and **communicate the changes to all households in the area (objectives)**.

As a project summary or mission statement, that's pretty watertight. And as you can see, the cascade from vision to benefit to objectives is there and they each clearly link back to one another right the way up the chain. Anyone reading this also has a clear idea of what the project will deliver, the reasons for delivering it, and the overall strategy that it sits within. All in well under 100 words. It's a very simple statement, but it will have necessitated a certain amount of thought and effort on behalf of the Sponsor and Project Manager to ensure the vision to benefit to objective principle is maintained.

This little bit of effort up-front means that you can now go out and deliver your project safe in the knowledge that you are properly set up for success!

SO NOW YOU HAVE THE WHY AND THE WHAT

The *how* is for the project team to work out and agree together. We'll get to that under planning.

THE EVERYDAY PROJECT MANAGER SHOULD ...

- Understand the over-arching vision (if applicable).
- Have clearly defined benefits, with associated measures that are agreed with – and owned by – the Project Sponsor (see Chapter 4).
- Have a short list of up to five objectives (no more), with defined success criteria, that are clearly linked to the project benefits, also agreed with the Project Sponsor.
- Remember: if you are not delivering the objectives, you are not delivering the project.

2

The Trade-Off: We Offer
Three Kinds of Service

Project management is delivering a desired outcome within an agreed timescale, for an agreed cost, and to an agreed level of quality.

THE HOLY TRINITY

So you have a project with defined objectives: great. Now what? At the start of every project, you will need to set some boundaries and expectations, especially with regard to the three things that define project management: time, cost, and quality (or scope).

Classic project management teaches us that, at its core, project management balances these three competing and complementary concepts. I recently saw a sign hanging in a project office that explains the balance and tension between these three nicely (Figure 2.1).

If you were looking for a quick summary of the tension that lies at the heart of project management, you could do a lot worse. And, of course, most people typically want all three.

This tension is typically represented as a triangle. This triangle is a way of showing the inter-connectedness of these three aspects of project management. Each is linked to, and has a fundamental relationship with, the other two.

In other words, you cannot change one without having an impact on (at least) one of the others (Figure 2.2).

FIGURE 2.1
Good, fast, and cheap.

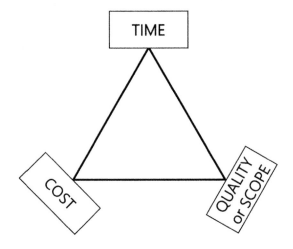

FIGURE 2.2
The time–cost–quality triangle.

A WORD ABOUT QUALITY AND SCOPE

In this equation, quality and scope are often used interchangeably, but they represent subtly different elements of a project, though they are clearly related. It is probably easiest to think of this corner of the triangle as "size of scope," or the amount you are being asked to deliver. As you will appreciate, if you are being required to deliver a product that is of a particularly high quality, it will have a corresponding effect on the time and/or the cost of that product. This doesn't just apply to projects but, to use an analogy, consider the difference in producing a hand-made gold-plated pocket watch versus a machine-assembled, mass-produced digital watch. You would expect the former to take longer, or cost more, or both, because the level of quality is so much higher.

Similarly, you would expect that building a house with four bedrooms, a bathroom, and a kitchen to be a quicker, cheaper project than a house with ten bedrooms, three bathrooms, and two kitchens. In this case, the build may be no more complex and the quality of the end-products may be no different. But clearly the *scope* of the second project is much larger.

In both the example of the watches and the houses, quality and scope are different, but if viewed in terms of *the amount the projects are being required to deliver*, they are grouped together. In practice too, the level of quality actually forms part of the scope. When you are scoping a piece of work, you would include within that scope some commentary on the quality expected. For example, if the project were re-fitting a kitchen, the scope would not simply specify that a sink was necessary, but whether the sink should be porcelain, or stainless steel, and whether it contained a waste-disposal or not.

In conclusion then, scope and quality are different but for most practical purposes, and particularly in terms of the Holy Trinity of project management, they can be viewed together. We'll see more on this later in the chapter.

WHAT IS FIXED AND WHAT IS A PRIORITY?

It's possible (sometimes even desirable) to prioritize one of these over the others, so let's have a look at what happens when you fix time, cost, or quality. Good – not to mention quick – decision-making is facilitated by understanding which of these is the priority on a project, as well as which of them – if any – is fixed. Typically, one or more of these will be fixed, and certainly one will be a priority for the customer; it will serve you well to establish early on which is which.

Where date, cost, or scope is fixed, challenge the assumptions to give yourself some flexibility. Why has that go-live date been chosen? What would be the real impact of moving it back a month? Has the budget been set at that figure because that is literally all the money available, or just because there is an expectation it can be delivered for that cost. Do we really need all the bells and whistles? Could we lose a piece of functionality without losing the overall result?

People have a tendency to artificially fix dates because they think it drives delivery, or because they have an (often unfounded) expectation of the time it will take. As a result, some customers will default to "I need it by this date" without a compelling reason. Use extremes to test whether this is a genuine or artificial constraint, e.g. "OK, if it will cost $50,000 more to have it by that date, do you still want it or are you happy to wait another month?" In my experience, cost tends to be the over-riding factor in most projects – though there are notable exceptions. For example, a wedding is a good example of a genuine fixed-date project.

In the same way, some tasks are of a fixed duration – they will take as long as they take no matter how many people you throw at the job. As a colleague once put it, "nine women can't grow a baby in one month."

Fixed cost usually relates to an available budget, or an agreement to do the work for a set price. If this cost has been committed (e.g. in a contract to deliver the project for a set price) then you will have little room for maneuver on cost. However, it's not unheard of for a customer who has rigidly fixed the price to "find" a little extra cash when there is some additional functionality they later decide that they want.

And in some cases, quality is non-negotiable – for example, a project to bring a new medicine to market must meet certain minimum legal standards of safety and testing, which no amount of cash or time will allow you to side-step.

AND I WANT IT YESTERDAY…

We've all heard that. But it is just one half of the conversation and, too often, the other half is not given airtime. The best project managers set themselves up for success by ensuring their stakeholders understand the cost/benefit trade-offs they are making – especially when they make demands on time, cost, or quality. So, the next time someone says they need something faster, by all means agree, but make sure that they understand that this will mean that the end result may not be of the originally agreed quality and may cost more to deliver.

Let's take a look at how we can meet changing demands on time, cost, and quality, with the corresponding trade-offs that would need to be made.

HOW TO GO FASTER, COST LESS, OR IMPROVE QUALITY

You have been happily working to deliver your project and you're on course to deliver on time. But in a meeting earlier today the bombshell dropped – either the deadline has been brought forward, the budget has been slashed or a higher specification is being demanded. What can you do to protect your project delivery? Here are some of the levers you might pull:

- **Throw people at it.** For certain tasks within a project the work rate is fairly constant, so increasing the people increases the amount of work done. For example, if the project is building an extension on a house, the "bricklaying" task has a constant rate. If you need to go faster you just increase the number of bricklayers.* However, you need to pay each additional bricklayer, so with each increase in speed comes an associated cost.
- **Outsource.** This is actually throwing people at it, by another name. Perhaps there is a part of your project that could be cut out and handed to another team or external agency to deliver, thereby freeing up your resources to deliver another piece of the project. For example, maybe one task is publicizing an event and you have planned that your team will spend an afternoon handing out fliers. This is the sort of discrete activity that could be handed over to another group or company, freeing up your team to work on another aspect of the event. Again though, hiring an external agency will have an associated cost that you will need to address.

---

* Note: there will be a point where you hit the law of diminishing returns because too many cooks are spoiling the broth. Using the above example, 100 bricklayers trying to work on the same 5 meters of wall will be highly counterproductive. Be aware of upper limits on adding resources to increase speed.

- **Find efficiencies.** Review the task list and see if anything can be dropped while still meeting the objectives (for more detail on this, see the next two chapters). Projects have a habit of picking up activities that are aligned to the overall project aims, but might not directly affect the project objectives and can be eliminated. By identifying these you may be able to make the plan a little leaner.

- **Sacrifice your contingency** (but not before reading Chapter 5). A good project manager will have included some scheduling contingencies within their plan so that even if something goes wrong, they can still maintain their original dates. This is to be guarded as though your life depends on it, but – in extreme circumstances – you may agree to give up your contingency in order to compress timescales. This can seem like an appealing option as it can be done with minimal impact on the cost and scope, but you are giving up your safety net. Do so at your peril, and as a last resort only.

- **Consider a phased go-live.** It might not be possible to speed up the delivery of the entire project, but perhaps a part of it could be delivered earlier, thereby reducing pressure on the rest of the project to speed up. For example, if the project is to deliver 20 finished products to a customer and they want it faster, would they accept five products sooner with the other 15 to follow?*

- **Reduce scope, part one: trade on quality.** One way to go faster is to trade on the quality of the finished deliverable. On building projects, one of the materials might be available quicker but would result in a poorer finish, or product life. Sometimes, this might be painless – we can paint the walls blue tomorrow, but green paint isn't available until next week. This will result in the customer getting something different from what they were expecting but in line with overall quality. Or you might refine the scope. If the project is to create a website, perhaps use stock photos rather than commission a photographer. The result will not be as well tailored to your client's needs, but may cost less and could be immediately available.

- **Reduce scope, part two: trade on scope.** If scaling back the quality of the project is proving difficult – or simply not worth it – consider

---

* Here again it is worth noting that there is potentially a secondary trade-off. In order to deliver five items sooner, you may need to divert resources and slow down production on the other 15. So you could end up trading time for time. Your customer will get five items sooner than agreed, but the remaining items later than originally agreed.

dropping whole chunks of it. To use the website example, let's say that the original plan was to allow people to sign in for special offers, but this was a nice-to-have function, and people can still buy things from the online store without it. By dropping the sign-in feature the website could be delivered faster or at a lower cost – or possibly both. An alternative to dropping scope could be to reschedule, so that your must-haves are delivered to the new deadline, while delaying the nice-to-haves to a later date. In the example above, the sign-in feature will still be delivered, but will be delivered at a later date, to be agreed upon. You've de-scoped it for go-live, but not from the project as a whole. As a result, the *overall* project may take longer to deliver, so there will be an impact on the schedule.

The following two diagrams show how the delivery of three widgets might change in order to prioritize the delivery of the first one. Here's the original plan in Figure 2.3.

In the original plan each of the widgets takes the same amount of time to build and test. It is agreed that Widget 2 can start being built in April once Widget 1 is comfortably underway. Widget 3 will begin building in May. Under this plan, Widget 1 is delivered in mid-June and the whole project is done by mid-August. The Sponsor decides they would like

Schedule	March	April	May	June	July	August	Sept.
Widget 1							
Build	▓						
Test		▓					
Deliver				◇			
Widget 2							
Build		▓					
Test				▓			
Deliver					◇		
Widget 3							
Build			▓				
Test				▓			
Deliver						◇	

◆ COMPLETION DATE: 14-Aug

FIGURE 2.3
Widget delivery, version 1.

Widget 1 to be delivered sooner – ideally before the end of May. The project manager reviews the plan with the team and they arrive at the following recommendation: there is a block of simultaneous activity in May and June with all three widgets having work done on them during this period. If we delay starting of work on Widgets 2 and 3, we could focus our efforts on getting Widget 1 built and tested more quickly, **but** we would not be able to achieve that and maintain the mid-August final deadline. The new plan looks like Figure 2.4.

Widget 2 does not start its build until Widget 1 is in testing, and Widget 3 does not begin until Widget 1 is complete. In May and June the team are not working on more than two widgets at a time. The *overall* project completion date is now early September, but Widget 1 is delivered almost a month earlier in mid- to late-May rather than mid-June. The Sponsor decides she is happy with this trade-off, even if it means the project won't fully complete until later than originally agreed.

- **Remove people from the project.** This is the counterpoint to "throw people at it," but if your budget has been reduced and you need to find cost-savings, one option might be to remove people from the project team. In this scenario, you go from two bricklayers down to one. The building will take twice as long to build but you have saved

Schedule	March	April	May	June	July	August	Sept.
Widget 1							
Build	▓						
Test		▓					
Deliver			◆				
Widget 2							
Build		▓	▓				
Test				▓			
Deliver					◆		
Widget 3							
Build				▓	▓		
Test						▓	
Deliver							◆

COMPLETION DATE: 03-Sep ●

FIGURE 2.4
Widget delivery, version 2.

the cost of an additional bricklayer.* This may also mean forgoing external agencies and doing the work in-house. You will save the cost of the agency, but you have limited resources yourself so the work will take longer as a result.

- **Consider other sources of funding, or ways to find additional resources.** If you are being challenged to keep costs down, is it feasible that another person or department might be willing to invest in the project, as they also have an interest in its delivery? This might not just be funding. Perhaps someone from another department or part of your life is willing to offer their time to help you deliver on time. It might be that the project you are working on offers a great development opportunity for someone and that their manager is willing to second them to you. However, *caveat emptor* applies. Sometimes offers of help quickly become a hindrance. Taking on a junior person as an extra pair of hands will require additional time for you to train or mentor them. Allowing for external investment means also allowing for external influence which is not always needed or wanted – and can be counterproductive. By all means, take the help that is offered, but do so with your eyes open. Set expectations with those offering help and be prepared to have your own expectations set in terms of any quid pro quo.
- **Increase or reduce testing cycles.** Testing – particularly in software development or product manufacture – is how you ensure quality. A typical software test cycle will involve internal testing (by the developer), external testing (by an independent test team), fixing the bugs, and then repeating. With each successive cycle, you – hopefully – reduce the overall number of quality issues that result. The same is true with product testing. And in both cases, the pass mark for testing will affect both the length of each test cycle and the number of cycles potentially required to pass. If a higher-quality product is required, increasing the number of test cycles will help assure this, but will take longer to achieve. Similarly, reducing the

---

* The eagle-eyed will spot that you will now have to employ the original bricklayer twice as long, so costs don't actually significantly reduce. This is true – to a point. As one former employer once said to me "bodies still take up heat and air." There is an overhead involved in employing anyone that does not directly translate into work done (e.g. employer taxes, welfare facilities, administration, office space, etc.), so fewer people means fewer overhead costs. Obviously, this is especially true at scale – the difference in overhead between 100 people and 200 people is significant.

number of test cycles in a plan will reduce the timescales but may put quality at risk.

- **Improve the underlying specification.** If an increase in quality is requested, it is worth looking at the constituent parts to see if by improving the specification of one item, the whole product is improved as a result. This may have an associated material cost. Or it might be that the higher the quality of the material, the longer the lead-time to get hold of it. But by altering one element, you may also save yourself a costly redesign of a whole project.

TWO LEVERS TO PULL

Ultimately, you will see that there are usually two levers you can pull. If the cost is fixed, you can change the time, but at the expense of quality. If the date is fixed, you can improve the quality, but it will cost you more. If the quality is paramount, you can reduce the cost, but it will take longer. A summary can be seen in Table 2.1.

THE COST OF CHANGE

Finally, any change will ultimately have a cost, be that in terms of money, time, or quality. Because every request to do things differently will require your time (and usually the project team's) to come up with the revised solution, re-plan, and adjust – or worse yet, write off – the work already done. Therefore, while change is a good thing (and the reason any projects exist!), you should do your best to ensure that change *within* a project is

TABLE 2.1

Balancing the competing constraints

I want to...	...but the scope is fixed	...but the cost is fixed	...but the date is fixed
Go faster!	Increase the budget	Reduce the quality	–
Get it cheaper!	Push the date back	–	Reduce the quality
Make it better!	–	Push the date back	Increase the budget

kept to a minimum. Similarly, where change is unavoidable, the project manager should seek to minimize the impact of any individual change to ensure the ship continues sailing smoothly.

AND THAT'S ABOUT IT

In many ways, you could end the book here (though I don't think the publisher will thank me if I do). As long as you grasp that project management is delivering a desired outcome within an agreed timescale, for an agreed cost, and to an agreed level of quality, everything else is, to a certain extent, simply building on those concepts. The rest of the book will tell you how to do things better, techniques to make delivery easier, and ways to manage each of those elements. The rest is about finesse though – once you understand that fundamental concept and spend your time managing the time, managing the cost, and managing the quality, well, you're already on your way to becoming a great project manager.

THE EVERYDAY PROJECT MANAGER SHOULD...

- Understand the competing challenges of time, cost, and quality.
- Agree up-front which of them will have the upper hand in decision-making.
- Use the levers available to enable the project to adapt to changes and challenges ("Go faster!").
- Keep an eye on changes to ensure they are kept to a minimum.

3

Project Scope: Defining the Requirements

In the previous chapters we saw how to define the project at a high level. The next chapter looks at the detail of a project. If this were a road trip, we have agreed the destination and whose car we're taking – maybe even stated an ETA. We now need to plan the detailed route, agree where we'll be making overnight stops and what snacks we want to bring for the journey.

THE FINAL LINK IN THE CHAIN

As the previous chapters have hopefully demonstrated, a project that has been properly conceived and thought about should have a clear link from vision to benefits to objectives. There is, however, one final link in the chain which is to the project scope, which is defined by the *project requirements*. As we moved from vision to benefit to objectives, the detail of what would be done became increasingly granular. In the same way, the step from objectives to requirements takes us into the detail of what needs to be delivered. The requirements can be thought of as the *specification*. That is, they specify what the end solution should look like. So, if the objective is to build a house with three rooms, a kitchen, and a bathroom, the requirements should tell you what color the walls will be painted and whether or not a dishwasher should be provided in the kitchen. Should there be a bath in the bathroom or a walk-in shower? Should the living room be carpeted, or have a hardwood floor? And to complete the chain, each requirement should relate to a specific objective and explain the manner in which the objective should be delivered.

The requirements help to define the *quality* aspect of the time-cost-quality triangle and ultimately define the full and detailed scope of the project.*

HOW DOES IT *FEEL?*

There are numerous ways of defining and recording the requirements, and there may even be multiple ways of defining them within the same project. Ultimately though, what the requirements are trying to do is answer the questions "How does the finished product feel?" and/or "How should it behave?" They are normally therefore specified by the person, or group of persons, who will be interacting with the finished output, with a final sign-off coming from the Sponsor. They should therefore be as detailed as the people specifying them need them to be. For example, the following requirements are all perfectly valid for an office carpet:

- The carpet in the office should be blue (to match corporate branding).
- The carpet in the office should be a dark shade of blue.
- The carpet in the office should be royal blue, stain-resistant, and fire-retardant.
- The carpet in the office should be *Carpets 'R' Us*, catalogue number #567-3B, a swatch of which can be found in the project office for reference.

As you can see, each iteration of the above adds another level of detail and specificity. It is up to the person specifying the requirements to ensure they have given a level of detail sufficient that they will be happy with the outcome. So, if you have simply said that the carpet should be blue, the project is successful when a blue carpet of any shade, pile, or quality is fitted. If the carpet is particularly important to you, it should be well specified in the requirements. Which brings us to the next point.

---

* It should be noted at this point that requirements definition and analysis is a discipline in its own right – Business Analysis. Large companies and projects will often hire one or more business analysts to work on the Requirements Lifecycle (and much else besides) during a project.

NOT ALL REQUIREMENTS ARE CREATED EQUAL

One common error that people involved in project delivery make is to treat all requirements as being of equal importance. When you have a – sometimes long and detailed – list of requirements, all laid out in the same way and not in any particular order, it is actually an easy mistake to make. One way to avoid making it is to include within the requirements some sort of scoring for each one, that tells the person delivering the project how vital each requirement is to the project's success. There are many ways to score requirements, but perhaps the simplest and most commonly used is the MoSCoW analysis. This system defines each requirement according to whether it is a *"Must*-Have," *"Should*-Have," *"Could*-Have," or *"Won't*-Have" (M, S, C, W, hence *"MoSCoW"*). Must-Haves are those requirements without which the project will have failed. Should-Haves will mean that it could be reasonably expected that these will be delivered if the objectives are to be achieved, but they are not "critical." Could-Haves are the bells and whistles which will not define project success, but could be considered for inclusion to improve the overall end-product. Won't-Haves are those things which, for the purposes of clarity, will not be delivered by the project. These are out of scope. For more information on out of scope items, and why it's important to declare them, see the section "What Is Out of Scope" below.

Table 3.1 shows some examples of requirements that fall into each category for an office move (Table 3.1).

As you can see from these examples, it would be reasonable to say the project has failed if people are unable to log on to their computers after

TABLE 3.1

Example MoSCoW requirements for an office move

Objective:	Move all IT equipment from the old office, installing it in the new office.
M	Every user should be able to log on to their computer in the new office and access their files.
S	Any specialist settings or functionality (e.g. access to a specific printer) should be migrated and not require additional configuration.
C	Any broken or faulty keyboards and mice should be replaced as part of the office move, provided they are clearly labeled.
W	The project will not replace any computers. Existing computers will simply be moved to the new office.

an office move (M). And it would be reasonable to expect that people who have specific set-ups that enable them to do their jobs should expect those set-ups to be mirrored in the new office (S). By the same token, it is not necessary – in order to deliver the objective – to replace broken keyboards and mice. But it would definitely improve the experience for those concerned and requires a small additional investment in the project to enhance the outcome. Hence, the Sponsor may decide to include it in the scope of the project (C). However, replacement of computers is a large capital investment with other strategic implications and so should not be included in the scope of this project (W).

The project team should focus their energies in that order, with the Must-Haves getting the most attention (and detail in the requirements). The Should-Haves should also be reasonably well-defined and represent a fair portion of the energy invested in the project. The Could-Haves should be a subject for discussion but should not hold up any of the main work. Needless to say, Won't-Haves must be noted by all involved in order to avoid wasting energy on activities that are not part of the project scope.

I MUST HAVE EVERYTHING

One of the biggest challenges when identifying the project requirements and signing them off is to ensure that the requirements are appropriately challenged. I cannot count the number of times I've reviewed requirements with a Sponsor only to reach the end and realize every single one has been declared a "Must-Have." Maybe that is the case sometimes, but if your list of requirements is more than, say, 20 items long, I would start to challenge whether every single one really is a Must-Have. That said, if a project Sponsor genuinely deems a great number of items to be Must-Haves, then logic dictates that the quality of the outcome is of paramount importance. This will have associated implications for both time and the cost of the project. It is the project manager's responsibility to remind the Sponsor that all scope items have a bearing on time and cost and therefore an extensive list of Must-Have requirements will have a related cost in terms of time, money, or both (i.e., CHEAP and FAST won't be GOOD).

LINKING BACK TO THE OBJECTIVES

As noted before, each of the requirements *should* relate back to an objective. In practice, you will often pick up requirements which do not neatly link back to the objectives. This is fine, but remember, if you're not delivering the objectives, you're not delivering the project, so treat these requirements with extreme caution, and challenge whether they are strictly necessary for the delivery of your project. These are often of the "while you're digging up the road" nature – that is, while your project is making changes in an area, it would make sense to do this too. From the example in Table 3.1, the "Could-Have" requirement of replacing broken IT equipment as part of an office move is a case-in-point. It clearly does not deliver the objective "Move all IT equipment from the old office, installing it in the new office" and could therefore be reasonably argued to be out of scope as it does not link back to the objectives.

It is a really good health-check to go through the requirements, once they have been compiled, and satisfy yourself that each of them has a link to one or more of your project objectives. If you find any that don't easily link, consider one of the three following approaches in discussion with your Sponsor:

- Consider whether the requirement is actually valid, or if it is just additional scope that has been picked up in the process. If it is not actually required, should it be re-classified as a Won't-Have?*
- If we agree that it is quite a good thing to include, but also agree that it does not contribute to the project objectives, it could be re-classified as a Could-Have (as in the example in Table 3.1). Thus, it has the appropriate level of priority – you agree to deliver it as a project, but the project will not have **failed** if it is not delivered. It also helps to make it clear that, if there is a decision to be made during delivery, efforts will be focused on the Must-Haves and Should-Haves before any Could-Haves that do not have a link to the objectives.

---

* Note that we re-classify it as a Won't-Have rather than simply removing it. Requirements that are rejected have a habit of finding their way back into your scope if you are not careful to manage them. Having a set of requirements that state "This item will **not** be delivered by this project" makes it clear for all, and prevents going over the same discussions again and again. It will also help prevent future disagreements about what would and wouldn't be delivered by the project.

- If we agree that this is actually a really, really good thing to include – and perhaps the project could not, in all good conscience, be considered a success if this *isn't* delivered, then perhaps the objectives themselves need to be reviewed and updated to include wording that allows for the delivery of this requirement as part of the objectives.

In any event, satisfying yourself that the scope of the project, as defined by the requirements, has a strong link to the objectives, will set you up for success and save you spending time unnecessarily working on delivering a requirement that contributes nothing to the objectives of the project.

WAYS OF SPECIFYING REQUIREMENTS

There is no single good way to specify requirements, and there are lots of different types of medium that can be used to define or draw them out. Some will be appropriate for specific types of project. For example, when you design a website, it might be easier to sketch out how you think it should look and annotate the drawing, rather than write a longhand list of requirements. In software development, scenarios called *use cases* are commonly used to examine how the software should behave under different conditions or for different users. Choose the method that best allows you to express what the end solution should incorporate and bear in mind it should also have some way of scoring the requirements to help you be clear which are the critical elements and which are the bells and whistles.

START WITH AN OUTLINE SCOPE

The most effective way of ensuring that what you define is aligned to your objectives is to start with an outline scope. For each objective, start writing out statements of what you would need to do to achieve it. For our earlier Community Recycling Project (Chapter 1) one of our objectives was:

- **"Provide recycling bins to all homes in the area."**

Think about what needs to be done to achieve this and you might end up with an outline scope that looks like this:

1. Undertake research to understand the number of homes in the area (and therefore the number of recycling bins required).
2. Produce a design for the recycling bins to be provided to the manufacturer.
3. Commission a supplier to manufacture the agreed number of recycling bins in accordance with the design which will be provided as an output of (2.).
4. Identify and implement a means of distribution that will ensure that all homes receive their allocation.

The outline scope is where we really start to define the activities we will need to undertake. Note that each statement begins with an action (undertake, produce, commission, identify).

Have you noticed that at each step of the way, all we are doing is defining the project in increasingly greater levels of detail? They're not big steps either, but we already have the beginnings of a plan here – a list of activities that we can clearly see will deliver the objective.

If you're having trouble figuring out the outline scope, imagine this. I have handed you a piece of paper with the objective written on it. Now you must describe to someone else what needs to be done in order to get there – provide them with a list of instructions or tasks that will get us there. That's your outline scope.

BUILD YOUR REQUIREMENTS FROM THE OUTLINE SCOPE

Once you have your outline scope, you then create the next level of detail: your requirements. The requirements do not state what must be done (like the scope does). The requirements specify what the end result of doing those things should look like. In the same way that we built our outline scope from the objectives, you now build your requirements from the outline scope. If we take the first scope item (undertake research), we now need to think about what the output of that activity should do. You might end up with a list of requirements that looks like Table 3.2.

TABLE 3.2

Example requirements list for a research paper

1.0	Undertake research to understand the number of homes in the area (and therefore the number of recycling bins required).	
1.1	The research paper should include a definition of the area boundary.	M
1.2	The research paper should include a description of the method used to arrive at the final figure.	M
1.3	The research paper should include a calculation of the total number of individual homes within the defined boundary.	M
1.4	The research paper should include a breakdown of the number of buildings surveyed, building type (e.g. apartment building), and how many homes within each building.	S
1.5	The research should identify and report the number of homes where recycling collections may pose a logistical challenge (e.g. a multi-story apartment complex, without an obvious location for residents to leave or store their recycling bins).	S
1.6	The research paper should identify existing community recycling facilities, as well as the number of homes within a 2-mile radius of each.	C
1.7	The research will not identify which homes use existing recycling facilities.	W
1.8	The research will not include a recommendation on how many recycling bins should be held as stock for replacement – that decision will be made by the Ops Manager later in the project.	W

With a little thought, and in a few simple steps, we've gone from a high-level objective, through an outline scope, to a detailed and well-defined set of requirements that will give us one of our scope items. By repeating this process for the remaining three scope items, you have a complete set of requirements for that objective. If that seems like a lot of work, consider two things:

- It is only as onerous as you want to make it. The process itself is straightforward, and is presented as a means of helping you structure your requirements so that the project is as well-defined as it can be. But you don't *need* to go to the level of detail specified above. You don't *need* to have a long list of requirements for each scope item. Maybe just pick one or two things that are especially important to you. If you're not worried about the rest, then, well, don't worry about them. Consider, though, how much better the output is when we provide requirements. Imagine if we did not bother with requirements for the research scope item above. We could still commission someone to "undertake research to understand the number of homes in the area" and they would go away and do that, and it's *just possible* that without any further guidance they will come back with just what you need. But by providing them with the eight simple requirements statements in Table 3.2, they have a much clearer idea of what they are being asked to provide, and what they give us will now very likely be just what we need.

- It is hopefully stating the obvious to point out that the better defined your requirements, the more likely it is that what the **project as a whole** delivers is exactly what is needed. The objectives are more likely to be met and the benefits of undertaking the project in the first place are more likely to be realized. The effort you put into project definition up-front hugely reduces the risk of misunderstandings – or straight-up project failure – later. Poor requirements definition is one of the main causes of project failure.

BASELINING YOUR SCOPE

You should sign off your outline scope with your Sponsor, as a high-level agreement on what the project will deliver. When the requirements have been fully developed (with the team, stakeholders, and the Sponsor), these too should be signed off by the Sponsor. This gives you a basis from which to measure change and keep a check on scope creep (which is discussed later in the chapter).

A FEW THINGS TO CONSIDER IF YOU ARE THE PERSON SPECIFYING OR REVIEWING THE REQUIREMENTS

- **Framing**. If you decide to list your requirements, a good way to frame each one is to begin each sentence with "The solution should…." By starting with these three words (or a variation) you avoid some common errors such as one-word, or too-vague requirements. For example, "Blue" is not a requirement. It tells us nothing and leaves plenty of room for misinterpretation. But "The (website) solution should have a blue background on each page" is far more descriptive and – importantly – useful to the person designing the solution.

- **Don't let perfect be the enemy of good.** One sure-fire way to slow down a project is to attempt to define the *perfect* set of requirements, or to put such a great number of requirements in that the solution will end up over-engineered for the purpose required. One way to avoid this is to challenge whether or not each requirement is properly related to an objective. Be ruthless: if the requirement doesn't relate to an objective, bin it. The other is to ask yourself, "Am I trying to create something perfect here, when good will do?" If you are, review the requirements again filtering for *good* rather than *perfect*.*

- **Constraints and objectives are not requirements.** In the same way that time and cost constraints are not objectives, neither should constraints or objectives be listed as requirements. This is (as with objectives) largely due to the specific language used. A Sponsor might require (small "r") the project to be delivered on time, but "The solution should be delivered on time" is not a valid Requirement (capital "R"). It doesn't tell us anything about the *nature* of the solution (i.e., how does it look and feel?). Similarly, one objective of the project might be to "Construct a workbench and lathe in the garden shed" but "The solution should construct a workbench" is not a valid requirement (unlike, say, "The workbench should be at least six feet long"). This might seem obvious but is a common mistake when defining requirements.

- **The requirements define the solution – not the other way around.** This is one of the trickiest traps to spot yet ironically the most important to watch out for. It occurs when people already have an idea in mind of the solution they want to see. As a result, they tend to *lead the witness* by building elements of their intended solution into the requirements. So, a requirement which states: "The solution should allow users to print emails" might seem perfectly reasonable. However, that might just be because the person defining the requirements has seen a similar solution that allows users to print

---

* Unless, of course, you want a **perfect** solution. But recognize that that is setting the quality bar as high as it can go and will have associated time and cost implications. Remember, the perfect solution is the one that does what is needed. Your project will be perfect as long as you deliver that.

emails. But what function is that providing? Could it be provided in another way? What is the question we are trying to answer? That is, what is the actual requirement? It turns out that the need to print was only so an audit trail could be kept. So perhaps the actual requirement is "The solution should provide a means of keeping an audit trail." Now, we haven't excluded the possibility of a print function, but this might also be done using an access log or time-stamps or by some other means. In any case, the requirement could still be met. At the same time, you have now afforded yourself more options for the solution – which is the correct way around. The solution should always follow from the requirement. As I like to put it: once you have a solution, it's much harder to find a solution. If you start with a solution already in mind, rather than a requirement, it becomes much more difficult to envisage different ways of solving the problem, and you risk missing alternative solutions that may be cheaper, quicker to deliver, or more fit-for-purpose. Moreover, projects that are solution-led (that is, the requirements are worked out retrospectively to fit a particular solution) run the risk of not meeting the objectives of the project or delivering the benefits as they have been arrived at from the ground up, rather than the solution resulting from the top-down cascade from vision to benefits to objectives to requirements.

- **Start at the end.** A good way to figure out the requirements is to start with the question: "For this project – what does finished look like?" and then describe the finished state. You will find you very quickly reel off a list of requirements. It is also a useful way, at the outset of a project, to consider the whole thing. It is important to have at the start of a project a way of assessing that the project is in fact finished.

- **Brace for resistance.** It is not an overstatement to say that a project with well-defined and clearly agreed requirements is already halfway to success. When you think about it, it stands to reason: the clearer you are about what you want, and the more time you put into ensuring the requirements are well understood, the more likely you are to achieve them. This ought to be a statement of simple fact, but you would be amazed at how unwilling people will be to actually specify what they want. Numerous reasons will be given – they're not interested in the detail; they don't have time to figure it out for you; they don't want to constrain themselves by committing, but want to keep things open so ideas can evolve – and they are all good reasons. All good reasons why projects fail. And none of them is a good excuse for not sitting down properly and defining what the project should be delivering. The counterpoint to this is that if you are not willing to sit down and clearly define what you want, you have considerably less right to complain when what is delivered does not meet your expectation. If I stamp my feet and say "I just want you to paint the room blue! Get on with it!" I can hardly complain when you paint the room dark blue and I had light blue in mind. But requirements gathering can be quite a dry and painstaking process (it can't all be fun and glamour). For example, you might be really excited at the idea of redecorating your living room, but the idea of going through umpteen carpet samples to choose the right one might fill you with dread or boredom and it definitely takes the shine off the exciting redecorating project. This is totally understandable, but time spent going through all those carpet samples will pay dividends when you have a room that you are really happy with – from carpet to ceiling. As a project manager (or the designated Requirements Gatherer for the project), expect resistance, but take time to explain why it's so important and how it will help the Sponsor get the very best result.

NOW YOU CAN BEGIN WORK ON THE SOLUTION

Only once you have a set of requirements should you begin working on the solution.* Best practice would be to have the completed set of requirements signed off by the Sponsor (definitely) and an end-user or super-user (recommended), who will be the ultimate user of whatever you're delivering (they may of course be the same person). You will then have a record of what was agreed, at a point in time, about what should be delivered. This is sometimes referred to as a baseline, and best-practice

---

* People familiar with agile project management may disagree with this statement. I accept it might be more accurate to say "Only once you have an *initial* set of requirements." This is to do with the difference between two key models of project management: (traditional) **waterfall** project management and (newer) **agile** project management. Both have their merits but, as stated in the introduction, for the purposes of *The Everyday Project Manager*, I have focused on waterfall project management. I believe it is the more appropriate model for "everyday projects."

project management puts controls in place to prevent deviation from what was agreed in the baseline (or rather, ensures that any deviation is done consciously). More on this later (see Chapter 7 Control mechanisms: Setting up your Project Governance).

But for now, let's say you have a signed-off set of requirements. These should be passed to the solution designer on the project. This might be an architect or engineer for a construction project, a software developer for an IT project, an interior designer for a refurbishment project… and so on. Whoever is responsible for designing the product that the project will deliver takes their instruction from the requirements. It will be for their particular profession to define how this should be done, what standards must be met, and what best practice looks like, but regardless of how the solution is arrived at, it must be capable of demonstrating that it has met all of the requirements.

TESTING THE REQUIREMENTS

To this end, your project should also include a period for testing the requirements to ensure that they have been met. In fact, you may even wish to factor in more than one test period to allow for changes to be made and re-tested. Early testing that reveals a missed requirement can save you a fortune in time and money later on in the project. The common-sense rule is that the later a problem is found or a change is made, the more costly it is to fix. So, if you can find a way to test the design before anything has even been built, you could save a lot of time and heartache further down the road. And the good news is, this can be really simple: as simple as looking back through the requirements once the design is received and doing a quick sense check that each of them has been addressed. You might be surprised how often this easy health-check is overlooked – with costly consequences later on.

As a minimum though, your project plan should include a period of testing after the solution has been delivered, but before it "goes live." This can be anything from a 30-minute inspection of a newly built extension, to several weeks spent software-testing, but it is essential that your plan allows for a period of requirements testing between the solution being completed and it being handed over to the customer. At handover, the

Sponsor (usually the end customer), should review their original signed-off requirements again, and confirm that they have been met.

SNAGS, DEFECTS, AND MISSED REQUIREMENTS

But what if they haven't been met? The key thing to consider is *in what way* has the requirement not been met? For this I find it useful to make a distinction between three ways in which a requirement has not been met. Different people have different terms for these and some use them interchangeably, but I use the following definitions:

- **Snag**. This is usually a cosmetic mistake or oversight. It is typically quite a minor thing to put right, but ought to be put right before the work is considered complete. So, for example, this might include some scuffing to the new paintwork as the builders removed their equipment or a crack appearing in the plasterwork as it set. It might be that one page on a website has the wrong background color, but the functionality is unaffected. It would be wrong to suggest that the project had failed on account of a snag, but you would still expect it to be put right before accepting that the work was complete.
- **Defects**. At the next level we have issues which affect the underlying functionality or fitness-for-purpose of the finished product. It will be a failure to correctly deliver on one of the explicit or reasonably implied requirements. They are not merely cosmetic (though there may be a cosmetic element to them), but have an effect on the overall usability. In other words, it is a mistake that can generally be corrected, but will require a little more effort and potentially some additional cost. For example, in a retail fit-out, the shop counter might have been cut a foot longer than was specified making it harder for the shop assistants to maneuver around it. Or there is a defect in the software that causes every third page on a report to be printed blank.
- **Missed requirements**. These are straightforward – quite simply, a requirement that has been explicitly stated (or that should be reasonably implied) has been omitted from the final delivery. In the complex, modern world there are countless ways that this can

happen (many of us have experienced the sinking, gut-wrenching horror of discovering the overlooked email, buried deep in our inbox, that requested something we have not now done).

Another way to think of this is that snags relate to *implied* requirements, defects to *stated* requirements not being properly realized, and missed requirements to, well, *missed* requirements, be they overlooked or forgotten. On a project to redecorate a room, the following might be considered:

- A snag: the room has been painted, but the paint has been scuffed in one corner of the room and requires touching up.
- A defect: the room has been painted, but the incorrect shade of blue has been used.
- Missed: the room has not been painted.

For a landscaping project:

- A snag: one of the chairs from the new garden furniture set arrived with a leg missing which needs to be re-ordered.
- A defect: the new fountain in the garden pond has been installed correctly, but the pump doesn't work, so some re-work may be needed to replace it.
- Missed: the flower bed at the side of the garden has not been planted, as it was accidentally cut off when the design was scanned and emailed through.

WHY THE DISTINCTION?

It is worth noting, that it doesn't *really* matter what you call any of these things – they are all a version of delivery failing to meet the requirements and should all, by rights, be rectified before the solution is accepted. The reason that it is useful to distinguish between these things is one of prioritization. At the point of handover you will usually be getting close to the end of the project or an agreed deadline. You will therefore – potentially – have a decision to make. Do you really want to die in a ditch about some scuffed paintwork in an area few people will see (and which the builder says was done by the electrician who says it was done by the plumber, and so on ad nauseam), or are you prepared to let that go in order to focus on the fact that none of the doors have handles on them?

Normally, you should prioritize the missed requirements, then the defects, and finally the snags. Bear in mind especially that a missed requirement is likely to mean the objective to which it is linked also gets missed, and the project is not considered to have been delivered (whereas a snag might be considered more fairly not to have resulted in the failure of the project).

COST TO RECTIFY

It is worth noting that, in a project where the requirements have been clearly defined and agreed, there should be no cost to the customer to rectify the snags, defects, or missed requirements. The requirements are the agreed scope of the project and will form the basis of any costs or quotes and any contracts or Statements of Work. To that end, a supplier is at best a little shady or immoral, and at worst in legal breach of contract, if they fail to correct the snags, defects, and misses at their own cost.

In practice, however – and certainly in relation to the snags – there is usually a bit of a trade-off to be had. Maybe the building contractor did put a small chip in the windowsill but, if you remember, they agreed to put an extra plug socket in at no extra cost, so there's some goodwill that can be exercised. Maybe it's not clear who was at fault for the missed flowerbed (perhaps you scanned it incorrectly, but could reasonably argue they should have noticed the drawing looked wrong or incomplete). You might decide to call it quits if they remove the cost of the flowerbed and you can plant it yourself at a more convenient time.

It is not unusual that in the heat of getting the job done, the odd thing might get missed, overlooked, or accidentally fudged. This can lead to all sorts of arguments, recriminations, and name-calling at the end of a project. If you failed to properly define the requirements it is much harder to argue your case – people have astonishingly short memories when they don't think they're getting what they asked for. Needless to say, the best way to avoid all of this is to have well-defined requirements that are agreed before the solution is designed or the work started. While there is no such thing as a perfect set of requirements and there will always be some room for interpretation, it takes a lot of the heat out the situation, if there is a clear set of requirements on record.

REQUIREMENTS FAILURE VERSUS REQUIREMENTS CHANGE

As you approach handover, one more thing to look out for is a habit some sponsors have for changing or, to put it more generously, "re-interpreting" the requirements. Again, if you have a signed set of requirements, these last-minute additions are much easier to counter. Look out for sentences like "I think it really *should…*" as opposed to "it says here we agreed that it *would…*." Some project managers choose to take a particularly hard line on these things – if it wasn't in the requirements it wasn't part of the scope of my project and I am therefore not obliged to deliver it. In most cases though, as with the cost rectification examples above, there is usually some space for discussion. However, always have the hard line at the back of your mind. The same applies down the supply chain. As project manager, you may have converted the requirements from your Sponsor into a Scope of Works for your building contractor (a Scope of Works is really just a set of requirements) to go hand-in-hand with the architect's design (which will also have been derived from the requirements). You need to remember the following guidelines,* whichever side of the divide you are sitting on:

- If it was clearly defined in the **agreed** requirements, then it should have been delivered. If it has not been delivered, then it is incumbent upon the delivering party to rectify that at their own cost.
- If it was not clearly defined in the **agreed** requirements, there is no obligation on the delivering party to deliver it.
- If the definition in the **agreed** requirements turns out to be unclear, or open to interpretation, then both parties will need to find a way to resolve the matter amicably (or possibly not, but this should always be the aim). This may mean reverting to mediation.

---

* …and they are just guidelines. Every engagement/contract will have its own terms and conditions as well as exceptions to and exclusions from the norm.

Finally, you'll notice I've emphasized "agreed" in the above. For the purposes of resolving disputes, it is essential that both parties agreed the requirements. The Sponsor must agree that the requirements accurately reflect what they want and that if the requirements are delivered they will be satisfied that the job is done. The Project Manager, or other delivering party, must agree that the requirements can reasonably be delivered within the agreed time and cost constraints before setting to work. Both should sign them off on this understanding.

SCOPE CREEP

Scope creep is the term for the many – *many* – ways in which the simple, easily deliverable job that you start out with grows into a monster. If you cast your mind back, I said that project management is *purely and simply* about managing the time, cost, and quality/scope (or words to that effect). Well, here's the quality/scope bit.*

SCOPE CREEP – AN EXAMPLE

Let's use the Outdoor Barbecue Area project mentioned in Chapter 1. The project objectives were to:

- Prepare the current area and undertake any enabling works.
- Create a design for the outdoor area that includes decking, a built-in barbecue, and outdoor lighting.
- Install decking and outdoor lighting.
- Build a new barbecue area in the corner of the decked area.

The project has been running a week or two; the area has been cleared and leveled and part of the decking is already down. One of the team working alongside the wall of the house realizes that on the other side of the wall is the family's hi-fi system and that if they drill

---

* For the sake of simplicity – I'll just refer to "scope" in this section, rather than quality/scope. But hopefully we understand the relationship between the two. (See the section in Chapter 2 A Word about Quality and Scope).

a small hole in the wall, they could run a wire and hook up some outdoor speakers. Everyone on site agrees this is a great idea. They also all remember that the objective of the project was to have an outdoor area for entertaining,* so this is perfectly aligned. One of the team has a cousin who works in a hi-fi shop and could get them a couple of relatively cheap speakers. They've made good progress so far and the work is looking to be a bit cheaper than originally planned so they agree to use some cash out of the budget to pay for them. Everyone agrees this is a terrific idea and during the lunch break, they're off to buy the speakers.

However, the cousin wasn't able to get them much of a deal, so the speakers were more expensive than they anticipated. And when they went to drill the hole in the wall, they realized there was a water pipe in the way (which was very nearly hit), and so they had to find an alternative route, creating a bit more work to make the outdoor wall good again. They also needed to remove a small part of the already laid decking (only a small part, so they figured it wouldn't take long to remove and put back) in order to run the cable to the final speaker location. Once the boards were removed, it started raining so work had to stop for the day.

The next day, the customer (Sponsor) returns from a business trip and checks in to see how progress is going. He is furious to see that where they had been ahead of schedule they are now behind. There is a hole in his wall that he didn't ask for and now needs to be made good. Furthermore, he's now told he needs to pay for some speakers that he never requested as he had always planned to use some wireless speakers that he bought at the airport during his business trip. The project is now over budget and behind schedule. But if they had just checked the objectives (or stuck to them) they would have seen that they were deviating. Had they stuck to the original plan, they would still be under budget and ahead of schedule.

But as you can see, each step of the way is just a minor transgression. That is, a small step away from the original plan, made in good faith, in the genuine hope of delivering additional value. This is why

---

* Nope! That was the *benefit*. But people don't always remember, particularly once work is underway. They're not being mendacious, it is just human nature. It's also a big reason a lot of projects go wrong.

it can be so easy to stray from the objectives, but also why sticking to them is so important. The gradual way that the objectives can sometimes be added to as in this example is known as scope creep.

VIGILANCE AND DISCIPLINE

Scope creep, then, is just a term to describe the subtle (or sometimes downright unsubtle) growth of a project's scope. Hopefully it should be obvious that scope creep needs to be carefully managed. If unchecked you will find the scope of your project growing which means that – all together now! – the project will cost more, or take longer, or both.

The best way to manage it is through vigilance and discipline. Ensure that your whole project team are clear on the objectives and requirements of the project. By having the scope clearly defined and shared among the project team, it will become obvious to anyone working on the project if a piece of work is in-scope or not. And if it's not, we shouldn't be working on it. The words "clearly defined" are important here. The more clearly you can define your scope, the less vague you can make each element, the less room there will be for interpretation, or for people to squeeze elements in that don't truly belong.

As project manager, you need to instill this discipline among your project team – the discipline to familiarize themselves with the scope and call out when work being done looks like it might sit outside the scope of the project.*

Then there is vigilance. By regularly reviewing progress on the project – going on site if that's applicable, or meeting regularly to get updates from team members on what they have been working on this week – you should be able to pick up on any scope that is creeping into your project. Earlier I talked about the importance of checking that requirements linked back to the objectives and this is another good reason to make sure that they do. If

---

* I would again point out, that these transgressions are usually done with good intentions, so I would advise against a heavy-handed approach. It is simply a matter of being clear about the scope and agreeing that we should not be working on anything that is out of scope.

you have satisfied yourself that the requirements link to the objectives, it should become even more obvious when something being worked on does not, and may be creeping into scope.

One of the more egregious ways in which scope can creep is through a Sponsor changing their mind about what they want *after* the scope or requirements have been signed off. This is more common than you might think and can lead to awkward conversations. It is not unheard of for a Sponsor to decide *halfway through the delivery of a project* that some new thing should have been in scope all along. Worse still, they might expect it to be incorporated while maintaining the existing delivery approach and without time and cost implications. If you have taken the time up-front to get a good scope together and have it signed off by the Sponsor then this might be a slightly uncomfortable conversation, but it should be a straightforward one. If you haven't got a well-defined scope, then the conversation becomes even more challenging, and you may find yourself having to accommodate this new requirement into a scope that you considered to exclude it. Even if you agree to accommodate the change, you should be at pains to show your Sponsor that it had not been included in the original consideration of scope (even if they consider that it should have been) and that expectations of time and cost will need to be adjusted.

Scope creep is therefore potentially very damaging to a project, but what if the scope is growing because you've identified new opportunities or additional value that can be added along the way, even though it wasn't formally agreed in the original scope? Not all scope growth is bad – some of it might considerably enhance the end result, or is just plain sensible to do even though it might have been overlooked when you first agreed the scope. Fortunately, project management gives us a mechanism for dealing with this type of scope growth.

SCOPE CHANGE – AND HOW TO MANAGE IT

If you, or one of your team, identify a change to the scope – be it scope creep or a straightforward request to include something additional into the project delivery, then there is no need to reject it out of hand. The thing to do is to capture the change and put it through a change management process – which is considerably less onerous than it sounds. We'll go into this in more detail in Chapter 7 Control mechanisms: Setting up your Project Governance.

WHAT IS OUT OF SCOPE?

Once a project gets out into the world, people (by human nature) will start to make all sorts of assumptions about what the project will be delivering. It is therefore useful to state not only what the project will be doing (in scope), but the things it definitely won't be doing (out of scope). It's amazing how often things that one person takes to be self-evidently out of scope are considered to be self-evidently in scope by someone else.

As an example, you are managing a project to roll out new company cell phones to the sales team. Question: will any training be included? For some people it would seem glaringly obvious that most people don't require training on how to use a cell phone. It's **obviously** out of scope. But that phrase – *most people.* Are there people on the team who perhaps aren't that comfortable with technology? It's rare these days, but not unheard of, for people not to own a cell phone of their own. Also, are there any special features or apps on the cell phone that might be *particularly* useful to a salesperson that should be highlighted for them to get the most out of the phone? Perhaps just a business card-sized cheat sheet with a few key features of the new phone would actually be very handy. Are all the calls made on the phone paid for by the company, or are they expected to make only business-related calls on the phone, with any personal calls made on their own phone? How should they prove which was which?

What first appeared to be an "obviously" out of scope consideration, is now a bit less obvious. Better then to be clear. If training is not going to be included, say so – expressly – in an Out of Scope section in your scope document or requirements.

In practice, most people struggle to put entries in an out of scope section, preferring to say that anything not explicitly defined in the requirements is out of scope. That's fair enough but, in some cases, it is worthwhile – for the avoidance of doubt – to declare certain elements as definitely out of scope.

YOU NOW HAVE A FULLY DEFINED PROJECT

With your requirements complete, you now have a fully defined project. Congratulations. Now all you need is a group of people to help get it delivered. In the next chapter we'll look at the project team and how it's composed.

THE EVERYDAY PROJECT MANAGER SHOULD...

- Start with a scope outline and then build a set of clearly defined requirements to ensure everyone is clear on how the end product should *feel*.
- Wherever possible, satisfy yourself that each requirement links back to one of the project objectives.
- Assign a priority to each requirement – you could score them from 1 to 5 in terms of importance, or use a system like MoSCoW ratings.
- Be vigilant for scope creep.

4

Roles and Responsibilities: I'm Putting the Team Back Together for One Last Job

All the world's a stage, and all the men and women merely players; they have their exits and their entrances; and one man in his time plays many parts.

William Shakespeare

WHAT ARE YOU LOT DOING HERE?

Having established what you are going to do, the next thing to do is establish the team that's actually going to do it. This is a lot more difficult than most people realize. It is one thing to assemble a group of people with a common goal. Successful project delivery relies on each of the people on the team having a defined role that is both clear to them and the others on the team.

One of the most common reasons I see for project issues arising (and indeed for outright project failure) is because those involved do not have clear roles and responsibilities. By establishing project roles with well-defined responsibilities and deliverables, you are setting your team up for success. This has several side-benefits too. By giving this some thought and ensuring all the roles you need to get the job done are filled, you satisfy yourself that all aspects of the project delivery will be covered by someone

– and if anything new arises, you will have a good idea of who you should be directing it to. The main benefit, however, is that people just work really well together (and are happier people) when they have a clear idea of what's expected of them and what they should expect of others. To that end, let's have a look at the more common roles that you will come across on the majority of projects.

KEY ROLES TO CONSIDER ON EVERY PROJECT (SPOILER: THEY MAY ALL BE YOU)

Let's have a look at the key roles that are common to most projects. Not all projects will have or require all of these roles, but most projects will have an element of them, even if the same person fills multiple roles.

The roles that every project needs to identify are:

- The Sponsor.
- The Project Manager.
- The Solution Designer.
- The Implementer.
- The Operational Owner.

There will be plenty of other roles, but every project should, at a bare minimum, identify these roles, as they are the people who will guide the project at various points in its lifecycle.

THE SPONSOR

One of the first questions to ask when identifying who will be the key players on a project is "who is the customer – for whose benefit is this being delivered?" Take note: this may well be different from the person who first brought the project to life or to your door. The customer for a project is known as the Sponsor. They will champion the project and will be the person who has (or should have) the most interest vested in its success. The Sponsor is typically a senior person within an organization (be that a team, department, or company as a whole), as they need to be empowered to make decisions and act with authority. Normally they will also be the person who is paying for the project (or who has acquired the funding for it); hence, the Sponsor is synonymous with the customer. Most important of all, the Sponsor owns, and ultimately receives, the benefits (see Chapter 1).

THERE'S ONLY ONE PROJECT SPONSOR

Wherever possible, there should only be one Sponsor. Since the Sponsor has the final say on project decisions, they need to be able to act autonomously to the greatest extent possible, so having two Sponsors (who may disagree) will inevitably slow the project down, or trip it up altogether. I have, however, found it necessary at times to have *levels* of Sponsor to recognize different levels of sponsorship within a company hierarchy. So, for example, a software upgrade might have the Service Desk Manager as the *Project Sponsor*, while the Chief Information Officer is the *Executive Sponsor*. Both have an interest in the project delivery and will receive the benefits, and both will need to be updated on progress and consulted for key decisions. They will both also be needed to champion the project at different levels of the organization. (It is usually easier for the CIO to get company-wide buy-in for the need for – and potential disruption caused by – a global software upgrade than it is for the Service Desk Manager). Make sure everyone is clear who the day-to-day Sponsor will be. They will be the person responsible for the majority of the decisions and guidance for the project and the one who engages most with the project manager and the project team. In the example given, where the different Sponsors represent different levels of the organizational hierarchy, there should be no more conflict, or indeed overlap, than there would be in their day-to-day roles. You are just reflecting that within the *project* organization. If, however, you find yourself with three Sponsors, I would suggest at least one of them is not a Sponsor at all, but a stakeholder. (See the section "Who Is *Not* on the Team?" later in the chapter).

This is especially true if you have two or more Sponsors who are peers within the organization. It is acceptable to have different levels of sponsorship to reflect different levels of a given hierarchy, as described above, but if you are drawing Sponsors from the same level of that hierarchy, you are setting yourself up for a problem. The most simple example of this is if the two Sponsors disagree on a point. Peers typically do not have the authority to over-rule one another. Ask yourself who would resolve such a difference of opinion. Guess what: that's your Sponsor.*

IF YOU ARE THE SPONSOR

If you are the Sponsor, your job is to work with the project manager to ensure the delivery of the project in order that you achieve the perceived benefits of undertaking the project. You should have a vested interest in the outcome of the project. You will be required to act as a champion for the project – you are its figurehead – and you will be called upon to represent the project from time to time. You should have sufficient authority to be in a position to help remove any roadblocks the project may encounter along the way, and the Project Manager will escalate issues to you in the expectation that you will resolve them.

You are the key decision-maker on the project and the final decision or casting vote on any issues will be yours. Therefore you should ensure you are both comfortable with making the key decisions and that you have sufficient authority. If you do not, you will need to strike up a working relationship (or develop your existing relationship) with the person who *is* authorized to make decisions and request that they either take over as Sponsor, or delegate authority such that you can make decisions on their behalf for the purposes of the project.

THE PROJECT MANAGER

The Project Manager is accountable for the delivery of the objectives of the project in line with time, cost, and quality expectations. It can be a complex role where you often feel like head chef and bottle-washer, confidante, motivational guru, accountant, friend, and foe all in the space of an afternoon. But if you are the Project Manager **no matter**

---

* This situation is not as unusual as you might imagine. Often, usually for political reasons, two people are put "in charge" of a project. If you find yourself in this situation, a Steering Group might be your best solution (see Chapter 7 Control Mechanisms and Chapter 10 In Extremis).

what happens, keep in mind that the essence of your job is to deliver the objectives according to the time, cost, and quality agreed and you will not go far wrong. This one piece of advice will stop you from getting drawn into numerous needless debates, blind alleys, and rabbit holes saving you time, irritation, and a lot of gray hairs.

You will need to develop a close working relationship with your Sponsor. The Sponsor needs to be able to trust that you have things under control and will deliver. Keep them updated regularly and always speak openly and honestly with them. This is *their* project after all – you are just managing the delivery – but they own it. By the same token, they are your go-to person for any issues that do not have a straightforward resolution. They should be wheeled out at important meetings (be that with senior stakeholders or members of the team) to act as a champion for the project. Others will *deliver* the project, but it is the project manager and the Sponsor that *drive* it, so you will need to become a close-knit, all-conquering team.

Good fences make good neighbors. Make sure there is a clear line between your responsibilities and those of your Sponsor – and that the Sponsor understands their role. This will make a world of difference and save a lot of frustration. Unchecked, Sponsors often have a tendency to "dive down into the detail" of the delivery. You need to remind Sponsors politely – but firmly – that delivery is your responsibility.

Beyond that of course, you will need to develop a good and close working relationship with each and every member of your team. Never underestimate the value of taking someone for a coffee. Often, the few dollars I've spent taking members of my team for an informal coffee to discuss one aspect of the project or another are among the best I've spent and have delivered more value for the project than some of the big-ticket items. In the world of project delivery, coffee is your friend.

You are also the glue that will bind many disparate elements of the project together, so you need to be visible, credible, and available.

Being visible means being on site, be that in the office or on an actual building site. Wherever the work is happening, you need to make sure you are a constant presence. There will be times, of course, when you need to chain yourself to a desk, or work from home, but to the greatest extent possible, you should be present. Remote project management rarely works in practice. That said, being visible applies even when managing remotely. Perhaps your delivery team is an outsourced group in another country. In this instance being visible means making sure you attend conference calls, or respond to emails in a timely manner. Make sure your team know you are there and visibly focused on delivering the objectives.

Being credible means, as the old adage goes, saying what you will do, and doing what you say. If you tell your team that you will have an awkward conversation that will ultimately move the project forward, then *have the awkward conversation.* And if you have no intention of having such a conversation, then do not say that you will. This is a really simple rule that, due to human nature and perfectly good reasons, can be very difficult to stick to. However, sticking to it delivers enormous value to you, your team, and ultimately to your project.

Being available means ensuring you are open to the concerns of others. Your metaphorical door should always be open. People need to feel able to talk openly and honestly with you, without fear of a backlash. If people are afraid to talk to you, or to deliver bad news, you will only find out about a problem when it is too late. This does not mean you should be a soft touch. Always make it clear that you expect great performance from your team and that failure to meet a target will be disappointing and damaging to the project. But if people feel they can't talk to you, they won't, and that could be disastrous. You will need to become a good listener. Don't indulge people who just like to whine – whining never helped anyone – but maybe take them for one of those precious coffees once a month. Often, there's something behind the complaining and you may unearth an issue that would otherwise have gone unmarked. On several occasions, I've taken a team member for a coffee and let them complain for a minute. By asking the odd probing question ("But why do you think that's the wrong thing to do?") rather than shutting them down, I have occasionally found that this person has thought of something I've overlooked, but just hadn't expressed that concern in a way that I thought was constructive.

Finally, you are not the expert. It is a common misconception that project managers are (or need to be) experts in the field where they deliver projects. This is simply not true. Project managers need to be expert at managing projects and nothing more. See the Subject Matter Expert (SME) role below for more detail, but I mention this as many people feel they are not qualified to deliver, say, an IT project because they don't understand computer networks. This is patently untrue. I do not know how to perform open-heart surgery, but this does not stop me from working for the NHS. Just not as a heart surgeon. I have delivered projects successfully for the financial services industry, law firms, and aviation corporations, across IT, training, process integration, and construction. I could not possibly be an expert in all these things.* But I am an expert in delivering projects. If you feel the need or pressure to be an expert, be an expert project manager. For your projects – get an SME.

IF YOU ARE THE PROJECT MANAGER

Build relationships with everyone on your team, and above all remember: if you do nothing other than deliver the objectives of the project in line with time, cost, and quality expectations, you will be a success.

THE SPONSOR AND THE PROJECT MANAGER

The Sponsor and the project manager are often confused as both can be seen as the *lead* person on a project. But as you can see from the above, they are actually distinct roles with different responsibilities. This is not to say that the Sponsor and project manager cannot be the same person. It's not necessarily even a conflict of interest, but **both roles still need to be executed**. If you are the Sponsor *and* project manager, do not neglect your duties as Sponsor in favor of your duties as project manager – and vice versa. The tendency when the role is combined is to confuse and prioritize the benefits over the objectives. When you think about it, the **ultimate** goal is to realize the benefits, and a combined Sponsor project manager will have that end goal in sight. This tends to be at the expense of the objectives so the danger with the combined role is the temptation to perform the *duties* of the project manager, but in order to deliver the benefits rather than the objectives. However, if you focus on the efficient delivery of the objectives, the benefits will follow. If you find yourself in the position of undertaking the combined role, consider this a cautionary note.

More often than not though, the Sponsor and project manager will be different individuals, reflecting their different interests in the project. Table 4.1 shows some examples of projects and their (potential) Sponsors and project managers.

---

* That is not to say I haven't picked up a few things along the way. It is not necessary for you to be an expert, but it is **essential** that you take an interest in and make time to learn about the area in which you are delivering your project.

TABLE 4.1

Examples of projects and their (potential) Sponsors and project managers

The Project:	An office move, within a building.
The Sponsor:	The Building Manager. It is in her interest that the move goes smoothly, with minimal impact to her tenants. The office move might increase the amount of available space she can rent (benefit), but she won't necessarily coordinate the works and logistics of the move.
The Project Manager:	The Building Manager's Assistant. The Building Manager delegates the running of the project to her assistant who will report on progress and escalate any issues that require the Sponsor's authority or seniority to resolve.
The Project:	An office move, between buildings.
The Sponsor:	The Chief Operating Officer. The move to new offices will reduce the operating costs of the organization, therefore the COO instigates a project to move offices, to be funded out of his annual operational budget.
The Project Manager:	The Office Manager. The move itself, though, is run by the Office Manager who oversees the transfer of equipment, computers, and furniture while also ensuring the office staff are kept updated.
The Project:	Building an extension on your house.
The Sponsor:	You. As the homeowner, you've decided it's time to extend your house. You've saved up and calculated the maximum and target budget for the build. You will need to move your family into rented accommodation for a period of the works, so maintaining the schedule is a top priority for you.
The Project Manager:	Also you. A flexible hours arrangement means you can fit the project management of the extension around your day job, so you oversee the works, ensuring the various building, plumbing, and electrical contractors are coordinated and on track.
The Project:	Replacing a marketing database with a new system.
The Sponsor:	The Marketing Director. The new system is much easier to use and will therefore save her team hundreds of work hours across the year, freeing them up to pursue other initiatives. It will also bring new functionality enabling the marketing team to reach, and maintain relationships with, a much wider customer base.
The Project Manager:	The Supplier. The supplier of the new marketing system has an interest in ensuring it is working optimally and also wants to ensure that the customer has a hassle-free transition. Therefore, as part of the package, they offer a project manager to support the transition and make sure the Marketing Director is happy with the new system.
The Project:	Creating a rail link between London and Manchester.
The Sponsor:	The Transport Secretary. As a government-sponsored national infrastructure project this will have oversight from several areas with ultimate responsibility lying with the Transport Secretary.
The Project Manager:	National contractor. The project is put out to tender. Out of an eventual shortlist of five national construction contractors, one is selected to manage and deliver the project.

THE REQUIREMENTS GATHERER

This is the person who pulls together all the requirements for the project. On large projects (and particularly in IT), this field is known as Business Analysis (see Chapter 3). The job of the Business Analyst is to work with the end customer to specify exactly how the end state should look and feel.

THE SOLUTION DESIGNER OR SUBJECT MATTER EXPERT (SME)

You wouldn't set out to climb Everest without a guide. In order to be successful you engage someone who knows the route up, what to bring, how much to bring, and who is able to find alternative paths if yours gets blocked. Enter the Subject Matter Expert (SME).

Every project requires an SME, but they can take several guises. On a building project, it might be the architect, on a software project it could be a developer, on a road safety project it might be a member of the Highways Agency or the Head of The Royal Society for the Prevention of Accidents. Indeed, depending on the breadth of your project, you may need to call on several SMEs at different points in the project.

The SME will be the person who guides you through the nuances and technicalities of the specific area you are working in, translating complex industry jargon into plain English. They will often be the person who designs the solution, or at the very least the person you trust to confirm that the solution is fit-for-purpose. For example, a contractor might provide a quote to build me an extension to my home, saying I need to include all manner of things I don't understand to meet building control standards, all of which add cost to my project. I need to have someone on my team (in this case, say, an architect) to confirm whether I really do need all these things.

As I've alluded to, the SME is going to be hugely helpful if the project hits a glitch as they will be the person best placed to come up with alternative solutions or workarounds.

On several projects I've managed, the SME has quite often ended up being my second-in-command. They have enough knowledge of the subject to make sensible decisions and usually have a vested interest in the project's success.

It is also worth noting that some projects touch on several disciplines and more than one SME may be required. Projects work best if there is just one project manager and one Sponsor. But you can have and, in many cases, *must* have multiple SMEs for a project to be a success.

IF YOU ARE THE SME

If you are the SME, be aware that you have been engaged because you have subject matter expertise in an area that others do not understand (or do not understand as well as you). It may in fact be a complete mystery to the rest of the team. Try wherever possible to avoid technical jargon or long explanations of the intricacies of your area (unless a detailed explanation is asked for). If you can take the key challenges and concepts of your specialist area and translate them into plain English, you will be considered invaluable and in very high demand.

THE SUPPLIER/IMPLEMENTER(S)

Of course, somebody will actually have to do the work! On a given project there may be several implementers requiring cooperation and coordination or there may be just one. On a construction project, you will have several contractors (builders, plumbers, electricians, carpenters, etc.). On a software project, you might have a team of developers who are writing the software. For an events project, you might have caterers, lighting and sound, printers (for brochures and publicity material), and possibly a specialist events team.

The implementer will have lots of input during the planning stage of the project assessing and advising exactly what needs to be done, how long it will take, and how much it will cost. Ensuring that the implementer has a clearly understood set of tasks to deliver and checking in regularly to follow progress and help remove any problematic issues will make for a smooth delivery phase.

IF YOU ARE THE IMPLEMENTER

If you are the implementer, ensure you have been given a clear scope that you understand. Confirm the budget and timescales and make sure you are happy that they are realistic. If you see any issues on the horizon, don't sit on them – let the project manager know as soon as possible. It's their job to ensure potential issues are fixed before they become real problems.

THE CHANGE MANAGER

If your project will have an impact on other people (and almost all projects do), you may at some point engage a change manager. This is the person who will help manage the transition from old state to new state. Their job will involve communicating with the affected parties to make sure everyone is aware of the changes. They will analyze training requirements and arrange training for those that need it (be that on a new computer system, or a new business process, or on how to operate the air-conditioning in a new building), perhaps even leading the training themselves. They might prepare quick reference guides, write press releases, or otherwise communicate to the media regarding the changes. Their role is to make the transition phase of the project as seamless as possible, but this means early engagement, wide consultation, and planning. A good change manager will leave people wondering what all the fuss was about.*

IF YOU ARE THE CHANGE MANAGER

If you are the Change Manager, work closely with the SME as, to a small extent, you will need to become a minor expert in the area yourself. The key to success is usually planning, and whereas most people on the project will tend to plan forward (working out what needs to be done, how long it will take, and arriving at a date), you will frequently be required to work backwards from an agreed *go-live* date.

---

* In this respect, it can be a thankless job. The mark of success is that nobody notices anything happened.

You will often be the voice of the project (hence the need to have a good understanding of some of the technicalities), so wide engagement across all stakeholders will be the key to your success.

THE OPERATIONAL OWNER

Most projects will create a product that is handed over upon completion to a person or team that will own and manage that product on a day-to-day basis (often described as *business as usual*). For example, once an extension is complete, the owner of the house takes control of it, owns it, and maintains it. If your project is to build a website for a client, the likelihood is that the client will own it and update it after completion. If the project is to install new seating in a public space, the local council will take ownership of it once installed and will be responsible for its upkeep. The operational owner is a key member of the project team as they have the predominant responsibility for ensuring the quality of the finished product. They will ordinarily set the quality standard that the product must achieve in order for them to take ownership of it.

IF YOU ARE THE OPERATIONAL OWNER

If you are the operational owner, ensure that you have a means of testing and assuring the quality of the finished product. You may wish to liaise regularly with the implementer during the delivery to ensure things are being built to specification. And you should certainly meet with the implementer at the start of the project to set out your expectations and the criteria you expect to be met before you will accept the finished product as complete. You should also have a plan in place to maintain the product once the project is finished.

AND THE REST

This is just a selection of some of the roles you are most likely to see or need on a project. But it is not intended to be exhaustive – there are many others. There will also be roles that are specific to certain industries (an IT project may have a Super-User for example, or a construction project might employ a Quantity Surveyor).

Make sure you consider at all times whether you have a need for a person on your team to undertake a specific role in order to deliver your objectives. It doesn't matter what their title is (a change manager might also be known as a Comms & Training Manager, but be performing a similar role). What matters is that you identify the requirement for someone to help you deliver the objectives of the project and assign that person a role, with specific responsibilities on the project team. And when I say you, I mean anyone on the project team. If you are working on a project team and think there may be a requirement for a certain skill on the team to deliver the objectives, then say so (see also the section Who's Missing from the Team? below).

Everyone on the project team should have a role in delivering the project objectives. If they do not, they are not helping to deliver your project. However, sometimes it will be politically necessary to have someone on the project team who does not actually have a project role. This is fine, but be aware of who is actually helping to deliver your project and who just has an interest. Do not confuse *project team* and *stakeholders* (even if a stakeholder happens to attend your project team meeting – see below).

COLLECTIVE RESPONSIBILITY

Many governments work on the basis of collective responsibility. The idea is that there will be a time for debate, but once a decision is made everyone supports it and works in its interests – even those who were opposed during the debate phase. The best project teams work in the same way. Open and active debate is encouraged, and a good project manager will endeavor to see that all sides are heard. However, once a decision is made, everyone on the team should get themselves behind it.

This starts with the objectives. If the project team have not bought into the objectives from the outset then you will really struggle to get buy-in for the decisions that get made along the way. It is therefore worth investing time at the start talking through the objectives and ensuring people fully understand and support them. This is predominantly incumbent upon the project manager, but should be done with the strong and vocal support of the Sponsor.

WHEN YOU ARE PERFORMING MULTIPLE ROLES ON THE TEAM

It is not necessarily an issue if you find yourself with more than one role on the team but it *is* important to realize which hat you are wearing and when. One of the more common role combinations in everyday project management is the combination of Sponsor and project manager. Needless to say, this is especially true of personal projects. If your personal project is to redecorate the spare bedroom yourself, you may well be acting as Sponsor, project manager, requirements gatherer, solution designer, and implementer. You will receive the benefit (a redecorated room) and will be funding the project (**Sponsor**). You will have overall responsibility for delivering the objectives (strip the existing wallpaper; prep and paint the walls; lay new carpet; and install fitted wardrobe) on time and in budget (**Project Manager**). You will have defined how you would like the finished room to look (**Requirements Gatherer**) and come up with the best approach for delivering it ("based on the last room I decorated, I now know that the carpet needs to go in last" – **SME**). And finally, you will be the person actually doing all the work (**Implementer**). That's fine. It is not unusual for a person to hold multiple roles but it is useful to recognize what is needed to fulfill each part of your job on the project and identify when you need to think like a Sponsor ("how does this affect my ability to achieve the benefits?") rather than an implementer ("is this actually within the scope of the job?").

BRINGING THE TEAM TOGETHER

The likelihood is that you will build your team up piece-by-piece, agreeing with individuals that they will be on the team and what you would like them to do for the project. However, it is well worth bringing the team together, as close as possible to the start of the project, and having everyone review the objectives together and walk through their role on the project.

It can also be helpful for each person to state what the inputs and outputs are for their role – in other words, what they need from the others in order to get their job done and what they will produce as a result. This is also helpful for people to understand the part they play within the wider team and give them a sense of the overall delivery and how their element contributes.

WHO IS *NOT* ON THE TEAM?

We've now covered everybody who is on the team, but – and this is a surprisingly important question – who is Not on the team? Because, believe me, on every project there will be people who have an interest, may even appear to be on the team, may even *insist* on being on the team, but are not on the team.

Here are some examples of people who are not on the team and how to manage them in a way that keeps them supportive while allowing the actual project team to get on with its work.

STAKEHOLDERS

Often you will have people who have a legitimate interest in the project, but do not have a role on the project team. These are your stakeholders and it's important to look after them and keep them updated. However, they have no place at project meetings and should not be allowed to influence the project direction or the work of the project team.

For instance, your parents might be legitimate stakeholders in your wedding. They might even have given you some money towards the big day. You will want to keep them informed of the plans (they need to know when it is and what to wear!) and perhaps let them know how their donation to the wedding has been spent. You might even seek their advice or opinions on what flowers to have or suitable music for the service. But this would not authorize them to pick up the phone to the caterers and have them change the menu (even if they think it entitles them to take that step). With stakeholders, the project manager needs to ensure clear lines are drawn and that they are kept informed of project progress. In fact, keeping stakeholders regularly informed is one of the best ways of managing them and keeping them at a sufficient distance to enable you to move forward with the delivery of the project. A legitimate stakeholder who is not kept in the loop may also quickly turn into a thorn in your side and start to cause problems. Conversely, a stakeholder who is properly engaged can often turn out to be a fantastic advocate for the project, making delivery even smoother and easier than it might otherwise have been.

Managing stakeholders is therefore vital to the success of a project and the best project managers are those that engage frequently with their stakeholders, while drawing clear boundaries with the project team. (There is another example of managing legitimate stakeholders at the end of this chapter.)

THE ILLEGITIMATE STAKEHOLDER

If the above is a legitimate stakeholder then, by definition, anyone else is an illegitimate stakeholder. And the world is littered with them. They usually fall into one of these categories:

- People who think they know (or may really know) something about what you're delivering, but are not on the team.
- People who feel they have been left out of your project, despite wanting a role because your project is an exciting or high-profile one.
- Senior managers or executives who believe their seniority alone gives them an entitlement (see below).

These people should be treated with caution, particularly as, in some cases, they may wield some power within the organization and, therefore, have some ability to harm your project, reputation, or even your career if they are not well engaged.

THE ILLEGITIMATE *SENIOR* STAKEHOLDER

Every so often, your project will attract the interest of someone further up the hierarchy but without a legitimate stake in the project. However, because of their position or authority within the organization they may feel empowered to request updates from you or even attempt to influence key decisions or the direction the project is taking. This can seem quite innocuous (and occasionally is), but if you have interest in your project at *any* level of the organization, you should be asking yourself if that person is a legitimate stakeholder. The tendency with the more senior figures is to assume they have a legitimate stake on account of their seniority alone. They do not. But you will find yourself on a political knife-edge dealing with such people and careful handling will be required.

HOW TO DEAL WITH THEM

One way to deal with this person is to identify a *legitimate* stakeholder who is also their peer – that is, a legitimate senior stakeholder (LSS) to counter the illegitimate senior stakeholder (ISS). If you're lucky, this could be your Sponsor, but if it isn't keep going up your chain of command (ideally via your Sponsor) until you find someone who is at the same level as this person. You will need your LSS to engage with the ISS on your behalf, listen to their comments, and feed them back into the project via the appropriate channels. They should also help you to keep the ISS at arm's length. It might be difficult, or even viewed as insubordinate, for you to ask the ISS to back off, but your LSS can do that more easily. In fact, by asking one of the ISS's peers to contact them specifically to get their input on the project, you should make them feel sufficiently engaged that they leave you alone and may even become a supportive influence.

As with all people who take an interest in what you're doing, the best tactic is to engage with them to understand what their interest is. This may be directly or via a colleague/manager, but engage you must or they will continue to cause a headache for you. Just remember, there is a reason they are interfering, even if it isn't obvious to you. Understand the reason, and the potential options for dealing with it will become clearer.

HAVING PEOPLE INSIDE THE TENT

Adapted from a quote credited to Lyndon B. Johnson about J. Edgar Hoover, "It's sometimes better to have people inside the tent pissing out, than outside the tent pissing in." Even when someone is not on the team, be conscious of when it is politically sensible, or even necessary to have them on the team. Just be aware that if they are not sitting in one of your required project roles, they are unlikely to be helping to deliver the objectives of the project, so don't rely on them for the success of your project.

IF YOU ARE AN ILLEGITIMATE STAKEHOLDER

Some people may have read this and reached the conclusion that they are in fact the illegitimate stakeholder. If that is you, don't worry, your intentions are almost certainly well-meaning. But consider whether you could be adding more value by assuming one of the defined or required project roles. And don't forget: your time is valuable too. If you have not bought into the delivery of the objectives, or simply don't agree with them, is there a better use of your time?

EXAMPLE – THE UNMANAGED STAKEHOLDER

You have been asked to manage an office move project. The people who work in the office are legitimate stakeholders. They are directly affected by the project and will need to bear a certain amount of disruption as a result of it, so it is a good idea to have them on your side. You might even seek their opinions on, say, artwork for the new office, or maybe have a competition to name the meeting rooms. In the other direction, you will need to keep everyone updated about the move date (which will probably be refined over time from "next summer" to "this July" to "three weeks from now on the 8th of July!"). You might share the seating plan for the new office so everyone knows where their desk will be and where the kitchen is for them to have their lunch.

However, none of these people are necessarily on the project team. They do not get to attend project meetings, have a say in how the project is running, or whether the move should happen on a weekday or over the weekend (though you might seek out a consensus of opinion on these things before the project team makes the decision that best serves the objectives of the project). What right does, say, Kevin from the Sales Team have to interfere? None. But Kevin might believe that he should be allowed to have a say because he is affected by the project, has been working at the company for 20 years, has always sat next to a window, and has strong views on what color the walls should be painted. Of course, a good project manager will seek to understand all these concerns and accommodate them wherever possible by managing the stakeholders, but in reality, on paper, Kevin has no such say over matters.

Consider though, what may happen if you fail to engage Kevin (or to keep any of your stakeholders updated). Kevin starts to grumble that the project is destined to be a failure because you haven't thought through the seating arrangements properly (even though you have). He's quite a forceful personality and soon has several members of his team being quite vocal about how the office move is a bad idea because it has been poorly conceived and managed. Soon the team are saying they refuse to move at all (in some organizations a union might well be involved). They start lobbying members of the management team (who until now, were blissfully unaware of any issues, and had assumed all was running to plan). Now they start taking an interest and asking all sorts of questions to satisfy themselves that everything has been properly considered. You are now so busy fighting fires and calming people down that you forget to confirm the move date with the removals company that is going to be moving the equipment. The move date eventually has to be put back a month costing the company thousands as they are committed to paying the rent on both properties until the move is complete.

This is not a completely ludicrous scenario. When people are not properly engaged, they tend to assume the worst and – whether they mean to or not – make trouble.

For the sake of completeness, imagine an alternative scenario where, in your role as Project Manager, you considered how to engage the office workers affected and make them feel part of the project. You book a meeting room for an afternoon, early on in the project, and host a drop-in session for anyone with questions about the move. Kevin drops in and asks if the seating plan has been completed. It has and, although he hasn't got a window seat, he is able to find out who has and you are able to help facilitate a swap. He's pleased with the outcome and ends up staying late the night before the move to ensure that his entire team has packed their belongings correctly in the boxes provided.

It's a small change, but makes a big impact. Stakeholder management does not need to be onerous, but it can make the difference between project success and failure – or the difference between good projects and great ones.

WHO'S MISSING FROM THE TEAM?

Finally, ask yourself whether anyone is missing from the team. Is there a key project role you've been unable to fill? Is there a particular expertise that would help you but is not available to you? It is worth taking note of who's missing and then adopting one of two approaches. The first option is to petition the relevant people to recruit someone into the role so that you have it filled. If this is successful, well done. You've closed a gap that might have endangered your project.

However, sometimes, for reasons of budget or availability, the person or tool that you need will remain out of your reach and so the second option is that you just have to accept it. That's fine – accept it, but always keep in mind that you have a gap in your team. This will need to be factored into your planning and will be a useful part of the narrative when you need to explain, for example, why the project will take longer than planned.

THE RACI MATRIX

One of the tools used by project managers to help define project roles and responsibilities is the RACI* matrix. RACI stands for **R**esponsible,

---

* Pronounced "racy." Though, let's face it, it's anything but.

Accountable, Consulted, Informed, and outlines the level of involvement each person should have for a given portion of the project or group of activities. Let's break down the RACI matrix below to explain this (Figure 4.1).

The first thing to consider is what we mean by responsible, accountable, consulted, and informed. These are important concepts, so it's worth spending time to get comfortable with them. I'm going to change the order below as I believe Accountable – Responsible – Consulted – Informed better reflects a descending level of importance, which helps a little when understanding the concepts.

Accountable: The accountable person is – surprise! – the person who has ultimate accountability for the activity. In other words, it is the person who will have to answer for its completion (or otherwise). This person has the ultimate right to take credit for the success but is also the person who must explain and take ownership for the failure. As one colleague put it to me, you can find out who is accountable by asking: "who do I fire?" Let's hope it never comes to that, but it is clear that you don't fire the builder if the house is badly designed. Accountability for the design lives with the architect (the builder has, after all, only built according to the architectural design they were given). Similarly, you do not fire the architect if the concrete mix is wrong and does not set (at this point the builder should be looking nervous). Accountability, in short, is where the buck stops. It is the person who has *ownership*. With accountability come privileges, of course. The accountable person will also be the decision-maker and approver (this might help identify them also).

Responsible: The responsible person is the person charged with actually *doing* something. They are the person who we are looking at to ensure the

Team Building Weekend	Colm	Simon	Chris	Liz	Sinead	Gosia
Book accommodation	A	I	C	C	I	I
Confirm attendees	I	-	I	A	I	I
Book speaker	C	A	I	-	R	-
Organise evening activity	C	I	-	C	A	-
Arrange transport	-	C	A	C	-	R

FIGURE 4.1
The RACI matrix.

job in question is done. Now, they may delegate that task, but they are ultimately responsible for ensuring its completion.

A NOTE ON ACCOUNTABILITY VS RESPONSIBILITY

In day-to-day language accountability and responsibility are often used interchangeably so the difference between the two (in a project world) is important to understand. This is made doubly difficult by the fact that the accountable person and the responsible person can quite often be one and the same.

A convenient and pertinent demonstration of the difference between accountability and responsibility is that old chestnut, the difference between the Sponsor and the Project Manager. The Sponsor is accountable for the project. The Project Manager is responsible for its delivery. If we go back to the principle of ownership, the Sponsor owns the project. They may even choose to replace the project manager, but the project goes on and they continue to own it. The Project Manager does not own the project* – only its delivery.

Consulted: This is the person, or group of people, with whom you need to have consulted in relation to the activity. You are not looking to them for a decision, or to undertake any part of the activity, but you may need information from them in order to complete the activity.

Informed: As the name suggests, this is anyone who should be kept informed about the task. They do not, however, have any responsibility for the task's completion, and we are not even seeking their opinion or expertise on the subject. They are simply informed. What format or frequency that informing takes is down to the project manager and the team, and will depend on the person being informed. It might be that you have agreed to let your project Sponsor know when a specific task has been completed. Or a member of the team might be informed about the outcome of a certain task, as it will then inform their task (for example, informing the decorator when you've agreed what color you're going to paint the walls, so they can then go and buy the paint).

---

* Counter-intuitively, and contrary to most people's understanding of the Project Manager's role.

THE TAKE-AWAY POINT

To bring this to life, let's consider the activity of ordering a pizza. Mom is paying (and as such refuses to order a Hawaiian and has the final call on pizza size). We've agreed that Dad should gather everyone's preferences and place the call. The kids have very clear ideas about the pizza they would like, and Mom and Dad have agreed they can decide on the order. Grandad doesn't like pizza, but would like to know when it's arriving so that he can heat up last night's leftovers which he'll eat whilst everyone else is having pizza so we can all eat together. So that looks like Figure 4.2.

PARTY WITH PIZZAS

Let's now expand that idea. It's Dad's birthday so Mom has decided to throw a family party where we've invited around 20 people. To cater, we've all agreed that we'll order pizzas, but some people might have specific dietary requirements or allergies, so Dad has decided to email everyone in advance to find out. He's also agreed to go to the supermarket to get the drinks. The kids have asked if they can decorate the house, which Mom and Dad have agreed to on the condition that they come up with a plan for the decorations and check it with Mom. As a courtesy, we're going to let the neighbors know that we're having a party. A RACI matrix for the party might therefore look like Figure 4.3.

THE NUMBERS GAME

For the record, for any activity **only one person** should be accountable. **At least one person** must be responsible. **Many people** can be consulted or informed – as you see fit.

Task	Mom	Dad	Kids	Grandad
Order a pizza	A	R	C	I

FIGURE 4.2
A take-away RACI matrix.

Family birthday party jobs	Mom	Dad	Kids	Grandad	Guests	Neighbors
Catering (order pizzas)	A	R	C	I	C	-
Catering (buy drinks)	A/R*	C	-	C	-	-
Create music playlist	C	A*	I	C	-	-
Agree guest list	C	A	I	I	-	-
Agree start/finish time	A	C	-	-	I	I
Send invitations	A	I	R	-	-	-
Put up decorations	C	-	A	-	-	-
Tidying up afterwards	A	R	R	R	-	-

FIGURE 4.3
Birthday party RACI matrix. * If a person is both accountable *and* responsible for the task, it is usual just to show the accountability; the responsibility is then implied. The accountable person is responsible by default – it's just that they will often need (or choose) to delegate that responsibility.

BEING CLEAR ON BOUNDARIES

Now, obviously, it's a strange family that pulls together a RACI matrix to agree who is doing what for a party but sometimes, even for relatively small projects, listing the jobs and agreeing who has ultimate accountability, who will be doing the work, and who needs to be consulted and informed is a very worthwhile task. All the more so if the people you are working with are not your family, but colleagues – possibly people you've only recently met. In that situation, spending a little bit of time (and it needn't be an onerous job) agreeing who is doing what and who should be involved, can save some heartache further down the line. And whilst it might seem a little anal to plot it out like this, people generally prefer it when their responsibilities have been made clear to them and they know the boundaries of what is expected of them. Finally, undertaking a RACI reduces accidental duplication of effort where two (or more) people think they are responsible for the same job and set off to do it, only to find out later (to mounting frustration) that it wasn't clear who *should* have been doing it.

THE PROCESS IS AN END IN ITSELF

I feel it is worth noting at this point that compiling a RACI matrix is an excellent example of a process that is – more often than not, in my experience – an end in itself. I have spent hours pulling together RACIs and debating who is responsible for what, only for the matrix to be completed, signed-off, and put in a drawer, never to be referred to again. There was a time when this used to frustrate and annoy me, but I later realized that sometimes you just have to go through the process – and that is the point. Don't get me wrong, having a signed-off RACI is a fantastic (sometimes essential) fallback. It will give you cover for decisions you make and allow you to remind people of what they signed up to. But frequently, you will go through the process and then put it to one side. Don't be disheartened by this. I'll let you in on a little secret – very often the output is not the point. It's about bringing people along for the ride and helping them to understand their responsibilities and accountabilities to the project. The RACI matrix – even if it has taken you *ages* to get right – is just a tool that helps you focus people on their role.* To that end – The Everyday Project Manager doesn't **need** a RACI matrix. It might be complete overkill for your project.† But in your head you need to be very clear who is accountable, who is responsible, who you should have consulted, and who you need to keep informed.

THE EVERYDAY PROJECT MANAGER SHOULD...

- Ensure everyone on the team has a role and knows their responsibilities.
- Be conscious of the difference between a team member and a stakeholder. Make sure you're aware of who *isn't* on the team and manage them appropriately.
- Have a RACI – at least in your head.

---

* See also: almost any project document, ever.
† That being said, for a free template, go to everydaypm.co.uk/templates.

Phase 2

Design and Planning

5

The Best-Laid Plans: Planning and Estimating Your Project

IF YOU FAIL TO PLAN...

Good planning is essential to the success of any project. The plan is not just a schedule of activity, but it is a communications tool that will enable you (and others) to understand how the project will be delivered. It will help to highlight which phases of the project will be busiest, or may require additional help. It will allow you to demonstrate that any dates you have committed to are in fact achievable and the logic that leads to that conclusion.

Project managers use all sorts of tools for planning, from a sketch drawn on a random page of a notepad, through to very expensive and sophisticated software packages that track hundreds of tasks simultaneously and give early warnings of issues that might not otherwise have been spotted. At the end of the day though, the tool you use doesn't matter anywhere near as much as the thought that goes into the plan. The very best plans will typically have some or all of the following features:

- The right level of detail so that it can both show and track the activities without becoming a job in itself to keep up-to-date.
- Some slack built in to allow for over-runs (especially on "critical path" items – see later).
- Clear breaks ahead of key activities, or investment points (to ensure over-runs do not put them at risk – see "firebreaks" later).
- Clear links between tasks that are dependent on one another.

PLANNING FORWARD VERSUS PLANNING BACKWARD

In an ideal world, all projects would be planned forward; that is, you identify how long it will take to complete all the tasks required, add some contingency, and arrive at a date which becomes your target. The alternative is to plan backward; you start from a target date or deadline and work backward to fit the tasks into the available time. If you are working on a fixed-date project, you will necessarily need to plan backward. This is not the end of the world and it happens all the time, but it comes with the additional risk that you are fitting the tasks to the time available rather than calculating the timeline to allow for completion of all the necessary tasks. And remember, even if you are working on a fixed-date project, not all of it has to be planned backward from that date. As much as possible, plan the tasks forward starting from today. In other words, where there is a possibility of planning individual tasks forward, you should. For example, imagine you are organizing the office Christmas party. The date has been set for December 18th, so you begin planning all tasks backward from that date. You might have a logic to your plan that looks like this:

- In order to hit the December 18th, the food order must be confirmed by December 11th.
- In order to confirm the food order by the 11th, I need to have received everyone's orders by December 9th (to allow a couple of days to check I've received them all and chase up any stragglers).
- In order to receive everyone's orders by the 9th, I need to have sent out the menu and requested their orders by November 18th (to give everyone three weeks to decide on their order and send it).
- In order to send out the menu on the 18th, I need to have received it from the supplier by November 17th.
- In order to receive the menu from the supplier by the 17th, I need to have requested it by November 10th (to allow up to a week for them to send it).

This is planning backward from the end date and gives you a series of "need dates" – simply the last date by which you need something. The plan now tells us that we need to request the menu by November 10th.

But let's say today is October 15th. Is there any reason this task couldn't be done today? No, there is not. And the task that follows it could then be brought forward too, so you plan to have received the menu by October 22nd and circulated it on October 23rd. This three-task sequence (request menu – receive menu – circulate menu) could be planned forward from today. So while the project as a whole is planned working backward from a date, individual tasks or sequences of tasks can still be planned forward. In doing so you create some breathing space within your project. If any of those three tasks is late, it causes much less of a problem because you're still some distance off your need date. Whereas before, by leaving it until the need date, you are left with very little room to maneuver if things go wrong.

In summary, wherever possible you should plan from the nearest date forward and not the end date backward.

FIXED DATE OR FIXED TIMELINE

A wedding is actually a good example of a project that could be planned either forward or backward. Anyone who's got engaged will know that the first question most people ask is "have you set a date yet?" Well, you could go about setting the date two ways. A forward planned wedding would start by looking at the objectives and requirements for the day. What sort of a wedding do the happy couple want? Should the wedding breakfast be a buffet dinner for two hundred, or a sit-down meal for nearest and dearest only? How many evening guests? Church ceremony or civil ceremony? Once the objectives and requirements have been established you can work out the tasks needed to deliver them. Once you've added a little breathing space you may end up calculating that in order to have the perfect wedding of your dreams, it will take approximately 18 months to organize. To give a little flexibility you give yourself a window of 18 to 20 months and set a target date.

A backward planned wedding might be set according to, for example, venue availability. Let's imagine that you've always had your heart set on getting married in the picturesque local church. It turns out a lot of other people feel the same way, so the venue needs to be booked in advance. So you book straight away, but you are now committed to the date and the remainder of the planning must work back from that.* Another example might be that you are planning to emigrate in two years and want to be married six months before that. You set a date 18 months from now and work backward from that date with all the tasks needing to fit within that 18-month window.

THE FIRST PASS – IDENTIFYING THE TASKS

It may help to think of a plan just as a to-do list with dates. While professional project managers and planners have all sorts of fancy tools at their disposal and ways of analyzing plans from multiple perspectives, at its heart, the plan is just a list of the things that must be done and the order in which they need to occur. Some of the best project plans I've seen and worked with are nothing more than this – and for all the tools at my disposal as a project manager, I always come back to "what needs to be done, and when?"

Your first pass at the plan should simply be an attempt to list out all the things that need to get done. There are plenty of ways to do this from listing them out in a spreadsheet, to writing them all down on sticky notes and sticking them to the wall so you can move them around. There is no wrong way to do this and there is only one right way – whatever works for you to get the plan straight in your head is the right way.

And, because I cannot overstate it enough, it is useful during this exercise to have the project objectives and requirements close at hand. I have even built project plans by listing the requirements at the top level, and then populating the tasks beneath each one (i.e., what are the things that need to be *done* to deliver this requirement?) This is a very solid way to ensure that the plan focuses only on the tasks required to deliver the project. However, even if you don't call out the objectives or requirements specifically within your plan, you should ensure that the task list is geared to delivering them. It is even a useful sense-check on a plan, as you enter each task to consider which requirement it satisfies.

---

* The eagle-eyed will have noticed that this is a slight fudge. If you have your heart set on a venue, this is not so much a date constraint as a must-have requirement (possibly even an objective) whose non-fulfillment will render the project a failure. However, fulfillment of the requirement *does* create a date constraint, so the subsequent logic remains.

A final point, which may seem obvious but is worth stating: the project plan should be worked up with your entire project team. Everybody on your team should have input into the plan and help to shape it. Plans that are worked up by the project manager in isolation are rarely successful. The role of the project manager during the planning is one of mediator and facilitator. Your job is to coordinate all of the input from your team into a single cohesive plan. This can be just as challenging as it sounds. Your role is also to ensure that the plan is realistic, achievable, and as lean as possible. This means it should not contain so much detail that it becomes unmanageable and also that there is not too much "fat" in the plan. Some contingency is always desirable, but if you believe a task should take one week, it is your job to challenge the person who says it will take a month (see also the section Estimating Tasks below).

The ultimate goal is to have a plan that is owned and bought-into by everyone on the team – the team owns the plan, the project manager manages it. This is also vital for accountability. If everyone was in the room when the plan was constructed, then everyone is accountable for its content and its delivery.

GETTING THE *LEVEL* OF DETAIL RIGHT

The appropriate level of detail will differ from person to person but always keep in mind that a plan that is too granular quickly becomes unmanageable. So, for example, if your project is to decorate a bedroom consider whether the following tasks:

- Drive to shop.
- Buy wallpaper stripper.
- Buy wallpaper paste.
- Buy new wallpaper.
- Buy stepladder.
- Drive home.

...might be better captured on the plan as the single task:

- Buy materials.

I'm exaggerating for effect, but you get the idea. Be careful not to confuse lists of things with over-arching tasks. Of course, it's just as easy to go too far the other way and have a single task:

- Decorate bedroom.

Obviously, the sweet spot is somewhere in the middle of these two extremes, but when you're planning a project it is easy to very quickly get lost in detail. In my experience, the first example (too much detail) is a much more common pitfall than the second (not enough detail). It's also worth noting that the second example with just one task, will be a really easy plan to manage – you can just tick off the one task when you've decorated the bedroom. This is clearly nonsensical, but the point is, the more detail you have, the more unwieldy and harder to manage the plan becomes. It will also be a lot less resilient to change, as small changes will require vast tracts of the plan to be rewritten.

As a rule of thumb though, the first pass should just be a brain dump – get it all written down. We can always summarize the tasks later.

THE SECOND PASS – ASSIGNING THE TASKS

The first pass has given you a list of all the things that need to be done to deliver the project. At this point, it is not unusual to become overwhelmed by the sheer volume of things that need to get done. But don't forget the first rule of project management: don't panic! The next steps will help bring order to that list and ensure that everything gets done. What's more: if you do have a list of tasks that is overwhelmingly long, then the chances are reduced that you have missed anything out – take solace from the fact that most of the things that need to be done have been captured.

Our next step is to start assigning all these jobs we've come up with to people. The aim of the game here is to make sure that every single task has an owner – and preferably a single owner. It might be that more than one person is carrying out the task – maybe even a team of people, but you want one person to own it overall. For example, a whole team of people might be involved in handing out fliers for an event, but you want one person to take ownership of the "handing out fliers" task, and report to you on its progress.

With your team, work your way down through the list and assign an owner for each task. Do not fall for the common temptation of putting your name against a task that no-one wishes to take responsibility for. If you ask the team who is going to own a task and the response is an awkward shuffling and then silence, the answer is not to put your name down. The project manager is responsible for the *overall* delivery, not the delivery of individual tasks.* A couple of suggestions if no-one is "biting." Plan A: if there is an obvious owner of the task and for some reason they just don't want to take it on, ask them if they would mind owning it for now until the correct owner is identified. Most people will not find this unreasonable. But make sure you follow up with them afterwards and understand why they don't think it should be them in the first place. You may either be able to convince them that they are the appropriate owner for the job, or they will convince you why they're not or why someone else is more appropriate (and you must then follow up with that person). Or you may not agree who should own the task, in which case go to…

Plan B: if there is no obvious owner (or the obvious owner does not agree that they are the obvious owner), leave the owner temporarily blank. This is an early warning that you may have a gap in your team that needs to be filled. It may be that you hadn't foreseen the task would be necessary and therefore hadn't recruited the appropriate person to your team. If you have several tasks without an owner, see if there is a theme that unites them. That might help make the missing role more apparent to you.

There are very few instances when the right person for the job is not apparent. If they are, your job now is – with the support of your Sponsor – to recruit that person. This might be easier said than done, as recruiting that person to your team could be as easy as having a conversation with them, or it might be as complex as undertaking a procurement exercise to hire an external consultant (having first secured the approval and funding to do so). In any event, the role needs to be filled as the task needs to be

---

* The exception, of course, is if you are also fulfilling another role on the team as well as project manager. But it is important to be really clear (in your own mind if nothing else) that you are taking on a task in your capacity as, say, subject matter expert – not just because no-one else put their hand up.

done. If the person required for the job is not apparent to you, your next step is to meet with your Sponsor and members of your team to discuss. Use the people around you and – as a team – work out who should be the owner of the task.

If you did have a long, scary list of tasks, hopefully it is starting to look a little less daunting now the work is being shared amongst the team, but we're not done yet.

With all the tasks assigned and everyone (hopefully) agreed about who will be doing what, we move on to the next stage.

In the following pages, I'll use a high-level example to demonstrate some of the key principles we'll be discussing. Emilio and Christian are undertaking a short project to redecorate a room. At this point they have written their list of tasks and agreed who will do what (Table 5.1).

THE THIRD PASS – SCHEDULING THE TASKS

The next job is to group and schedule each of the tasks. Again, there are multiple ways you could approach this – you could identify all the tasks that can start this week, then next week, then in the next month, etc. You could print off a calendar and assign the tasks to various days within the calendar. In almost all cases though, it is useful to have some sort of representation of the timeline and to put your tasks onto it. Often, the easiest way of all though is simply to work down your list of tasks and put start and finish dates against each one.

TABLE 5.1

Task list for decorating a room

Task	Owner
Buy materials	Emilio
Cut new skirting to fit	Christian
Remove wallpaper	Emilio
Remove skirting boards	Christian
Sand down walls	Emilio
Prime walls	Emilio
Put new wallpaper up	Emilio
Install new skirting	Christian

TABLE 5.2

Task list with dates assigned

Task	Owner	Start	Finish
Buy materials	Emilio	Jun-01	Jun-02
Walls			
Prepare walls			
Remove wallpaper	Emilio	Jun-03	Jun-03
Sand down walls	Emilio	Jun-07	Jun-08
Prime walls	Emilio	Jun-10	Jun-11
Put new wallpaper up	Emilio	Jun-11	Jun-14
Skirting			
Remove skirting boards	Christian	Jun-04	Jun-04
Cut new skirting to fit	Christian	Jun-04	Jun-04
Install new skirting	Christian	Jun-15	Jun-15

Unsurprisingly, there are a number of computer programs and websites out there to help you to do this. Many will turn your tasks and dates into something called a Gantt chart which is a neat, visual way of showing each of the tasks, their duration, and the order in which they occur.* These tools will convert a list such as the one shown in Table 5.2 into something more like the Calendar view in Figure 5.1, or the Gantt chart view shown in Figure 5.2.

As we can see straight away, this lays things out in a much more "user-friendly" way and allows us to see a couple of additional things. With each day represented as a column, by looking down the columns you can see which works are due to take place on any given day. This is a great help, as you can now see if any given day has too much work to achieve and where there may be clashes between areas you are working on. For example, it is now easy to see that we have decided to remove the skirting boards and cut the new ones to fit on the same day. That might be fine, but there's only one person doing both jobs – maybe just one of them is achievable in a day, so we might wish to consider moving one of the tasks forward or backward in the plan to make it more achievable. It also shows us that we've allowed two whole days to buy the materials, when maybe one is enough. It's easier to spot when represented visually like this though. Let's have a look at how

---

* For an updated list of suggested free online tools, go to everydaypm.co.uk/tools.

June

	1	2	3	4
	E: Buy materials	E: Buy materials	E: Remove wallpaper	C: Remove skirting C: Cut new skirting
7	**8**	**9**	**10**	**11**
E: Sand down walls	E: Sand down walls		E: Prime walls	E: Prime walls E: Wallpaper up
14	**15**	**16**	**17**	**18**
E: Wallpaper up	C: Install new skirting			

FIGURE 5.1
Calendar view of tasks.

Task	Who?	01 June	02 June	03 June	04 June		07 June	08 June	09 June	10 June	11 June		14 June	15 June
Buy materials	Emilio													
Prepare walls	Emilio													
Remove wallpaper	Emilio													
Sand down walls	Emilio													
Prime walls	Emilio													
Put new wallpaper up	Emilio													
Remove skirting boards	Christian													
Cut new skirting to fit	Christian													
Install new skirting	Christian													

FIGURE 5.2
Gantt view of tasks.

a couple of other simple techniques can be used that will make this plan even better.

INCREASING SCHEDULE MATURITY

One way to improve the robustness of your schedule is to map the dependencies between the various tasks. That is to say: are there any tasks in your plan that rely on another task having been completed? So, for example, we can't sand down the walls of the room we're redecorating until we've first stripped the old wallpaper off. If we map the dependent tasks in the above example, our plan now looks like this: Figure 5.3.

Task	Who?	01 June	02 June	03 June	04 June		07 June	08 June	09 June	10 June	11 June		14 June	15 June
Buy materials	Emilio													
Prepare walls	Emilio													
Remove wallpaper	Emilio													
Sand down walls	Emilio													
Prime walls	Emilio													
Put new wallpaper up	Emilio													
Remove skirting boards	Christian													
Cut new skirting to fit	Christian													
Install new skirting	Christian													

FIGURE 5.3
Schedule of tasks with dependencies mapped.

Task	Who?	01 June	02 June	03 June	04 June		07 June	08 June	09 June	10 June	11 June		14 June	15 June
Buy materials	Emilio													
Prepare walls	Emilio													
Remove wallpaper	Emilio													
Sand down walls	Emilio													
Prime walls	Emilio													
Put new wallpaper up	Emilio													
Remove skirting boards	Christian													
Cut new skirting to fit	Christian													
Install new skirting	Christian													

FIGURE 5.4
Optimized schedule of tasks.

By doing this, we're able to demonstrate another issue with our original plan (indicated by the star in Figure 5.3). We can't put the new wallpaper up until we've finished priming the walls. We had previously scheduled the two to happen together, but by understanding the dependencies, it becomes clear that one (or both) of these tasks will have to move if our plan is to be achievable.

The plan shows us that there is an opportunity to move the "prime walls" task to one day earlier, June 8th, but that we can't move it any earlier than that as it is itself dependent on the "sand down walls" task. After a bit of tweaking though we can arrive at a completely optimized plan, that removes all clashing tasks, respects the dependencies, and still comes in by our original target date: Figure 5.4.

So, a few simple principles applied and already we can be feeling much more confident in our plan. When shifting the tasks to remove clashes, though, I have not taken account of the fact that two people are working on the job, so certain tasks can be run in parallel. If we parallel-run certain tasks, we'll almost certainly achieve some time-savings as a result.

If we re-draw the plan, with Emilio's tasks represented by the squares and Christian's by the diamond pattern, the plan could now look like this in Figure 5.5.

Task	Who?	01 June	02 June	03 June	04 June	07 June	08 June	09 June	10 June	11 June	14 June	15 June
Buy materials	Emilio											
Prepare walls	Emilio											
Remove wallpaper	Emilio											
Sand down walls	Emilio											
Prime walls	Emilio											
Put new wallpaper up	Emilio											
Remove skirting boards	Christian											
Cut new skirting to fit	Christian											
Install new skirting	Christian											

FIGURE 5.5
Schedule of tasks with parallel activities.

By assigning tasks in a logical way, we've saved three days on our original estimate. We've been able to bunch certain tasks together, but there is one more opportunity to be exploited and we'll use it to explore the concept of the critical path.

THE CRITICAL PATH

The critical path defines the absolute minimum time a project can take. Put simply it is the longest sequence of dependent tasks through your project, i.e. the tasks that define the absolute minimum duration (from start to finish) of your project. This is a really important concept when it comes to understanding how important certain tasks are to maintaining the overall schedule. Here is our plan again, but with the critical path filled in solid (Figure 5.6).

Tasks on the critical path will delay the entire project if they themselves are delayed. They therefore have particular importance when you are trying to keep to schedule. If "sand down walls" over-runs, it has a

Task	Who?	01 June	02 June	03 June	04 June	07 June	08 June	09 June	10 June	11 June	14 June	15 June
Buy materials	Emilio											
Prepare walls	Emilio											
Remove wallpaper	Emilio											
Sand down walls	Emilio											
Prime walls	Emilio											
Put new wallpaper up	Emilio											
Remove skirting boards	Christian											
Cut new skirting to fit	Christian											
Install new skirting	Christian											

FIGURE 5.6
The critical path.

knock-on effect on the subsequent tasks in the chain, ultimately causing the whole project to over-run.

The checkered tasks, however, are not on the critical path. If, for example, "remove skirting boards" slips by a day, it will have a knock-on effect to the subsequent tasks, but will not delay the project overall. This is useful to know as we now understand which tasks have some "float" (that is, they can slip in the schedule if need be without affecting the overall project duration). Obviously, the amount of float is limited and if they slip too far, they will delay the overall duration of the project – at that point they will become critical path tasks themselves.

If we return to the critical path for a moment: "buy materials" and "remove wallpaper" are first and second in the sequence. Technically, the tasks themselves are not dependent (you could remove the wallpaper whether or not you have bought the materials). So there is no task dependency, but there is a resource dependency as we are relying on the same person to do both jobs so, in that sense, one cannot be started before the other has finished.

By understanding the critical path, we have highlighted two opportunities. We have some scope to re-arrange the non-critical path tasks while maintaining our overall schedule **and** by removing the resource dependency (by re-assigning the "buy materials" task to Christian instead of Emilio), we can reduce the number of items on the critical path. Emilio can get started on removing the wallpaper and sanding down the walls because these tasks are not dependent on materials having been bought. As Christian is not on the critical path we can use some of the "float" in his activities to free him up to buy the materials.

We could now end up with a fully optimized project plan that looks like Figure 5.7.

And, just like that, we've managed to shave another day off the plan!

When managing your own projects, look to the critical path if you wish to save time on the overall project. Saving time on individual tasks is always a good idea if possible, but only tasks on the critical path will bring in your end date.

As a final note on the critical path, beware of a common misuse of the term. I regularly come across people who state that an activity is on the critical path when it is, in fact, just a critical activity. Which, in turn, usually means it is just critical (read: important) to them. In other words, when someone uses the critical path as a means of inflating a task's

Task	Who?	01 June	02 June	03 June	04 June		07 June	08 June	09 June	10 June	11 June		14 June	15 June
Buy materials	Christian													
Prepare walls	Emilio													
Remove wallpaper	Emilio													
Sand down walls	Emilio													
Prime walls	Emilio													
Put new wallpaper up	Emilio													
Remove skirting boards	Christian													
Cut new skirting to fit	Christian													
Install new skirting	Christian													

FIGURE 5.7
Optimized critical path.

importance or urgency, it might just be worth checking that the end date genuinely is endangered by this task's late delivery and, if not, why the person in question is so keen to increase its priority.*

PUTTING THE FLOAT BACK

Having removed your float from the plan, it is sensible to allow yourself a little contingency by putting some float back in. We know the work can (at least in principle) be done in 7 days, so it makes sense to allow 8 or 9 days for the full job to be done. Life, and the world of project management, is full of surprises, and by allowing an additional day or two at the end it means you are a bit more prepared when the unexpected happens. It also means that if any individual task slips you have some capacity to absorb the delay. A project that promises to deliver on June 7th, but comes in a day late is deemed to have failed. But if you promised June 8th and deliver according to the plan you know you can achieve on the 7th, it's a resounding success. Note: this is not an encouragement to lie or to bulk out your plan with so much fat that it is unnecessarily over-long. However, a small, considered amount of float that allows you to be prepared for the unexpected is a good plan.

As a very crude gauge of how much float is sensible, pick the one item that is most likely to run into difficulty. Have an educated guess at how much time an issue with that task could cost you – and either halve or quarter it depending on how likely you think it is to happen (very likely – halve it; not so likely – quarter it). This is a very crude measure, but fine

---

* For more on this, see the section on "False Urgency" in Chapter 8.

for The Everyday Project Manager and you have a quick and easy means of estimating your float.

ESTIMATING TASKS

If you believe a given task should only take a week, but the person delivering that task insists it will take a month then you should challenge the estimate. Ask them to explain why the task will take as long as they say – there might be a good reason you hadn't considered (e.g. it would normally take a week, but the factory closes for two weeks at Christmas which will push delivery into the New Year).

But remember: you are not the expert. You are within your rights to challenge and satisfy yourself that the estimate you are being given is correct, but in the event of a stalemate, I suggest two courses of action:

1. Defer to the expert, but:
2. Make it clear that they are fully accountable for delivering to that timescale – they own that estimate, and will be called upon to explain if it is not achieved.

It is common sense in projects to maintain a level of pressure to ensure things are done in the shortest time possible. If you allow six weeks for a task, guess what? It will take six weeks. If you put a little pressure on and ask that it is delivered in four weeks, there's a chance you will find that it can be delivered in four weeks. But there is a balance to be struck. It is bad practice and bad management to stress people out and force them to deliver on an unrealistic timescale simply for the sake of it. So listen to what the team is telling you and make a judgment.

BROADLY RIGHT VS PRECISELY WRONG

It is alright, and often desirable, not to be too precise. It is far better to say that the project will be delivered in July and deliver it in July, than it is to say that the project will be delivered on July 15th at three in the afternoon, only to deliver it on the July 18th and the project to be considered a failure. Or, to put it another way, it is better to be broadly right than precisely wrong.

Obviously, the earlier in the project lifecycle you are, the more acceptable it is to be vague. If it's July 15th and you're still saying that the project will be delivered "sometime in July" people may be within their rights to request something a bit more specific. This is where planning horizons come in.

PLANNING HORIZONS

This is the idea that the farther you are from an event the less precise you are able to be about its timing. People will often pressure you to give precise dates and times for events, and sometimes that's entirely fair. Within a single plan there may be varying levels of specificity. When talking about dates, it makes sense though to be more specific the closer you are to the event. When I'm planning a project, as a rule of thumb, I use the planning horizons shown in Table 5.3.

Bear in mind, this is just a rule of thumb and will depend greatly on the nature of the project being delivered and the demands of the various stakeholders. Timings could be described minute-by-minute during an event but only be accurate to the month further out. I've been involved in one project that lasted over two years but where the timings during "go-live" were so important that an entire 72-hour period was planned by the minute.

TABLE 5.3

Planning horizons

The task is due to happen...	I should know (at least)...	And ideally...
Today or tomorrow	Morning, afternoon, or overnight	What time
In the next month	What date	Morning, afternoon, or overnight
In the next three months	Which week	What date
In three to six months	Which half of the month	What date
In six months to a year	Which month	Which half of the month
A year from now (or more)	Which quarter	Which month

Consider, for example, what a plan for a wedding might look like. Let's say the wedding is in August. In January of the same year, your plan might say "Book florist during March." The precise date of the wedding will be known, but in January the timings of the day might be completely unknown, or only sketched out. But as the year progresses, timings will get more refined, to the point that by late July, the wedding day itself may have quite precise timings, e.g.

- Service: 2pm.
- Drinks and canapes: 3pm.
- Wedding Breakfast: 4pm.
- Band arrives and begins setting up: 6pm.
- Evening guests arrive: 6.30pm.
- Music starts: 7pm.

After the main event, timings might become less refined again:

- Return hired suits: August 23rd.
- Honeymoon: August 24th–September 7th.
- Wedding list delivery: September 14th.
- Write thank you notes: by end of September.
- Chase photographer if wedding photos not received: first half of October.
- Close wedding savings account: November.

PITONS AND FIREBREAKS – PUTTING IN YOUR FAILSAFE MECHANISMS

When putting a plan together I like to employ two failsafe mechanisms – one from the world of climbing and one from the world of firefighting. They are pitons and firebreaks respectively.

Pitons. Though they are not used so much these days, climbers used to use tools called pitons as a safety device. Pitons are hammered into the rockface that you are climbing and then attached to a rope. The idea is that, should the climber fall, they will only fall as far as the last piton, which arrests their descent. The analogy for project planning is hopefully clear. It is a good idea to identify your own "pitons" within your project plan that act as a point you will fall back to if there is an issue, but not go beyond. A good example of a project piton is requirements sign-off. Once your requirements are signed off, there is no need to go back through early email discussions about what might or might not be the best way of achieving the solution. Archive them and when there is an issue go back to the signed-off requirements to resolve it. You might find it useful to create some pitons if there are no obvious ones, for example, by identifying where you could sign-off certain stages of the delivery. Let's say you're staging a sports tournament. Your pitons might be:

1. Venue confirmed.
2. Fixture list finalized.
3. On-site catering organized.
4. Stewards and first-aiders booked.
5. Final teams confirmed.
6. Go/no-go decision.

As you can see these are each major milestones from the project plan. They are re-phrased in the above example as a finished state, so there might be various tasks that relate to organizing the on-site catering, but once all have been concluded you will have hit your "on-site catering organized" piton. Using the analogy, you can hammer that piton into the mountain, know that that part of the climb is done and carry on to the next piton. If something goes wrong during the next bit of the ascent, don't panic and go back to square one. Just go back to the last piton and see what has to be done from there.

It's also good for the project manager's state of mind to be able to mark off key points in the project's development to maintain a sense of forward momentum. It is helpful to draw a line under large chunks of work and be clear that they are complete. On larger projects (or perhaps I should say projects with larger budgets), these may represent significant achievements along the way that are worth recognizing and celebrating with the team – perhaps organize a social activity to celebrate the completion of the milestone. It goes without saying that this will also help feed team morale and give them a sense of achievement and pride in the project's progress.

Firebreaks. One technique used by firefighters is to create a firebreak. This is a tract of land that is stripped bare of any trees, vegetation, or foliage to prevent the spread of fire and allow firefighters a chance to bring it under control. A firebreak might also be used to protect valuable pieces of infrastructure from being affected by a fire nearby. And this is precisely how they should be used in your plan.

If there is a particularly key date that you want to ensure has an increased chance of being hit, it is sensible to put a bit of float in immediately before it. That is to say, ensure there is a gap between the last task prior to your key date completing and the key date itself. An example of where this might typically be used is with a launch date. Let's say the project you're managing is a restaurant opening. You sit with the team, plan out all of the activities in sequence and arrive at a date of August 22nd. This is the earliest date on which the restaurant could be opened, as all the preceding tasks will have completed by that date (Figure 5.8).

Obviously though, you will be doing a lot of publicity surrounding the launch and you will need to be communicating the launch date ahead of time. It would be costly (and embarrassing) to advertise an August 22nd Grand Opening, only for one of the preceding tasks to over-run and the launch date to become unachievable. Therefore, as project manager you discuss with the Sponsor (the restaurant owner) setting the launch date at September 12th – this gives you three weeks of float in case of any issues or delays on *any* of the tasks that precede the launch.

However, the restaurant owner is unable to start making money until the restaurant is open, so whilst she accepts the logic of having a gap, she feels three weeks is too much. You review together the likelihood (or risk) that any of the tasks beforehand will over-run and eventually set a launch date of September 5th. You have negotiated a two-week firebreak into your plan, which means you can be that much more confident of hitting your Grand Opening (Figure 5.9).

Task	JULY				AUGUST				SEPTEMBER			
	Wk 1	Wk 2	Wk 3	Wk 4	Wk 1	Wk 2	Wk 3	Wk 4	Wk 1	Wk 2	Wk 3	Wk 4
Main construction work												
Restaurant fit out												
Furniture on order												
Crockery & cutlery on order												
Hire staff												
Finalize menu & send to print												
Advertising campaign (local paper & radio)												
First grocery order for launch												
GRAND OPENING							★					

FIGURE 5.8
Restaurant opening – high-level plan.

Task	JULY				AUGUST				SEPTEMBER			
	Wk 1	Wk 2	Wk 3	Wk 4	Wk 1	Wk 2	Wk 3	Wk 4	Wk 1	Wk 2	Wk 3	Wk 4
Main construction work												
Restaurant fit out												
Furniture on order												
Crockery & cutlery on order												
Hire staff												
Finalize menu & send to print												
Advertising campaign (local paper & radio)												
First grocery order for launch												
GRAND OPENING										★		

FIGURE 5.9
Restaurant opening – with firebreak.

Notice that in the new plan, the grocery order has moved within the firebreak – this is because it is linked to the opening itself, which has moved. You do not want fresh groceries sitting around for two weeks while your firebreak elapses. You also don't want to pay your staff if the restaurant isn't open, so we've shifted the hiring period back a couple of weeks, whilst keeping it outside the firebreak. In other words – be aware of other tasks that might be affected by implementing the firebreak and move them accordingly, while aiming to keep the firebreak itself clear.

Some people are uncomfortable with having a plan that contains a lot of activity, followed by a stretch of nothing. Some will also worry that if others realize there is a two-week gap, that will make it alright to take their foot off the gas as they know the project can withstand a small delay. There are a couple of ways to deal with this.

The first approach works if you have a close and trusted team who are as committed to achieving this as you are. You need to be clear that the firebreak blocked out in the plan is *your* contingency, not theirs. You will still be holding every project team member accountable for the dates they originally committed to, and they will need cast-iron explanations if they are not met. You may even choose to incentivize early/on-time delivery or penalize late delivery. If you're using third parties, you could even have the delivery dates written into the contract. In truth, it is worth doing all these things *anyway*. In the case of the restaurant opening, it might be a small family-run restaurant with family and friends all joining in to get the job done. In this case, just being clear that it's a contingency period should be sufficient as everyone will be personally invested in hitting the dates anyway.

The alternative approach would be to consider what will be done in that period if it turns out not to be required for over-runs. Speak to the Sponsor

– "If you were granted a bonus two weeks right before launch, what would you do with them?" It would be ridiculous to have everything ready and just let the restaurant sit empty for a couple of weeks with nothing going on. Instead, identify what *could* be done in that time and summarize it up into one or two tasks, for example "Pre-launch tasting sessions and final preparation period." You know, and the Sponsor knows, that this is actually your strategic firebreak and you must both be prepared and happy that any activity in this period could be dropped if a previous task over-runs. The plan now has the firebreak in there (by another name), but without the risk that anyone else working on the project will see a gap in the plan and believe it therefore doesn't matter if their activity delivers a week or so late.

GO/NO-GO DECISIONS

It is worth considering another failsafe mechanism that is slightly different in nature from your pitons and firebreaks. Pitons and firebreaks are break-points within the plan that create additional security to protect against issues, should they occur. A go/no-go decision is a break-point that is there to confirm consensus at key points that the right thing to do is either to proceed or to stop. It is simply a meeting, or a phone call, or even an email that confirms certain key people are committed to the next course of action.

You might insert a go/no-go decision before a major tranche of funding needs to be committed, or before going public with a policy, or before the launch of a new piece of software. In any case, the go/no-go is there as a final check that all the necessary criteria have been met for the project to proceed. It is also there so that those in positions of authority can confirm their awareness and support for progression to the next stage (or have the opportunity to halt it). These can be nerve-wracking calls indeed, but they are a hallmark of responsible planning – giving those in power the option to stop before we are all committed to a course of action.

This means there are some important things to consider as project manager:

- **Make it count.** You do not require a go/no-go for every last decision on the project. These decision points are reserved for major waypoints where a commitment is going to be made. Ask yourself if a (potentially irreversible) commitment is being made at this point. If it is, a go/no-go may be appropriate.

- **What are the decision criteria?** As I say, the purpose of this is to establish that all the criteria for "readiness" to move to the next stage have been met. It is important, therefore, to agree in advance what those criteria are – what constitutes "ready?" For example, if the go/no-go is for a software launch, the criteria might be:
  - Has the software successfully passed all its testing cycles? *(Software testing manager to answer).*
  - Have all the people identified as requiring training on the software received the appropriate training for their role? *(Training manager to answer).*
  - Has the IT helpdesk been briefed that the software is being rolled out tonight and have additional people been rostered on to ensure any queries are quickly answered? *(IT Helpdesk manager to answer).*
  - Have all users of the software been advised (via at least one email) that it is launching tomorrow? *(Communications manager to answer).*

As project manager, you should circulate the criteria in advance and get agreement that if all of these come back as a "yes," then the software can launch (we have a "go"). Bear in mind that some of these answers may not be a clear-cut yes or no. The software might have passed 56 out of 57 test cycles, but the one it failed is a minor glitch and the project should probably proceed anyway – this is the call that you are asking people to make, and it might require some discussion and thought. Therefore it is important that you have the right people.

Who needs to be there? It won't surprise you to hear that as a bare minimum, the Sponsor should be involved. Also, several people may have an input to the conversation but they will not necessarily be decision-makers. So in the example above, the managers for software testing, training, IT helpdesk, and communications will all need to be involved in the discussion, but none of them are likely to be the authorized decision-makers for whether or not the software launch goes ahead. As I stated, the purpose of the call is to get agreement from the senior stakeholders in the project, specifically those people within the organization authorized to give you the go-ahead, that they are happy to proceed, while giving them a final opportunity to ask questions or put the brakes on. If you're wondering who that is, picture a scenario where you go ahead without someone's knowledge. Who is the person that picks up the phone to you to ask "Why on earth wasn't I informed?!" Discuss attendees with your Sponsor – you don't want a cast of thousands (there is no need for the entire project team to attend, much as they might like to), but ensure you have given the attendees some thought and that the people in the room *can* make the call you're asking them to make.

For the go/no-go decision itself, remind everyone of the decision they are there to make – you might want to give a brief update on progress-to-date if appropriate and an overview of where the project is at. Then simply work through the criteria to establish whether the project can proceed or not. Go round the room and ask each person in turn if, based on the information shared, they are happy to proceed.

If so, you have a "go." You now have authorization to continue with your plan. You can go back to your team and carry on, following your project plan.

If not, it is a "no-go" – for now. Before the meeting finishes, ensure that you establish next steps. Make sure you have a clear understanding of the reasons it was a no-go. These are the things you will need to address before reconvening (if appropriate) for a subsequent go/no-go. Importantly, don't be disappointed if it is a no-go (easier said than done, I know). It is important to remember that although everyone would prefer a "go" decision, a "no-go" demonstrates that you have implemented a sensible, responsible approach to project planning, avoided a botched launch or a potentially disastrous outcome, and ensured that when you do "go," it will be all the better for having made the necessary adjustment you must now make.

MILESTONES AND MILESTONE MANAGEMENT

The final step on the road to your project plan is to identify your milestones. These are not tasks themselves, but are key checkpoints along the way, that will confirm (or not) that the plan is on track.

Most plans will have some natural milestones that will be immediately obvious as key dates – "Go-Live," for example. And, of course, *all* plans will have a final "project complete" milestone. If there are not many natural milestones, insert new milestones at the end of major activities, phases of work, or to mark certain achievements. You should use the milestones to delineate the main phases of activity within the project. The idea is that the activities that sit between milestones have some flex and might move, provided the milestones themselves do not. You might therefore have a "product enters testing" milestone at the start of your test phase and a "product passes testing" milestone at the end of your test phase. Now, anything that delays the "product enters testing" milestone affects your entire test phase and every subsequent activity, so while individual tasks prior to that milestone might flex up or down, you need to ensure that the milestone itself does not move. Similarly, the activities between the two milestones (effectively the test phase) might be re-ordered or tweaked, and that's ok, as long as the "product passes testing" milestone is unaffected and can be maintained.

Once each milestone has been achieved, you have a clear marker of project progress and a sense of how well the project is tracking against the original plan.

Some pointers for selecting your milestones:

- Clearly, the number of milestones will be dependent on the size of your project (and indeed your plan). That said between five and ten milestones should be more than sufficient for most projects. More than that and you're starting to get too far into the detail. You will also be reducing the amount of flexibility you allow yourself.
- It is sensible (though not essential) that any milestones you select sit on the critical path, as a delay to a critical path activity delays the whole project.
- Always put a milestone after a firebreak, never before.
- Do not base milestones on durations, e.g. "Three months from launch." The fact that you are three months from launch tells you nothing about project progress. Milestones should be based upon the completion of activities.
- The same applies for percentage complete, e.g. "Design 50% complete" should not be a milestone. How are you assessing when something is half done? Or 75% done? Milestones should mark **full completion** of activities only.

Task	JULY				AUGUST				SEPTEMBER			
	Wk 1	Wk 2	Wk 3	Wk 4	Wk 1	Wk 2	Wk 3	Wk 4	Wk 1	Wk 2	Wk 3	Wk 4
Main construction work	▓	▓										
CONSTRUCTION COMPLETE		◆										
Restaurant fit out			▓	▓	▓							
FIT OUT COMPLETE						◆						
Furniture on order			▓	▓	▓	▓						
Crockery & cutlery on order	▓	▓	▓	▓	▓	▓						
INTERIOR COMPLETE							◆					
Hire staff			▓	▓	▓	▓	▓					
ALL STAFF HIRED							◆					
Finalize menu & send to print					▓	▓						
Advertising campaign (local paper & radio)			▓	▓	▓	▓						
First grocery order for launch									▓			
Tasting sessions & final preparation period								▓	▓			
GRAND OPENING										◆		

FIGURE 5.10
Restaurant opening plan with milestones.

Milestones are traditionally marked on project plans with a diamond. Here's an example of our restaurant opening project plan from earlier with the key milestones now included (Figure 5.10).

Once you have selected your milestones you should review and agree them with your Sponsor. Once they are agreed with the Sponsor, they are "baselined" – that is to say, you, as project manager, agree that these are the dates that you commit to hitting. All the underlying tasks are for you to manage but are in your gift to adjust. However, you are committing to your Sponsor that the milestone dates are the ones that you will deliver against.

Following on from that logic, the Sponsor is welcome to take an interest in the detail and logic that leads to each milestone, but those underlying tasks are yours to manage. You should absolutely go through the detail of the plan with your Sponsor and agree the milestones. But once you have, the Sponsor should only be holding you accountable for those milestones, and should not really be concerning themselves with the detail. Your job is to report – honestly and transparently – to the Sponsor on progress toward achieving each milestone.*

The other side of this coin is where a milestone has moved, irredeemably, beyond your grasp. If something happens that means a milestone will no longer be achieved, you **must** escalate it to your Sponsor (at least). As you have committed to achieving the milestones, you should be reporting on

---

* Note also that if you are using a third-party supplier to outsource some (or all) of the delivery, you should request a milestone plan from *them* and hold *them* accountable for delivery to the milestones (effectively you are the Sponsor for their element of the delivery).

them, perhaps assigning a level of confidence or Red–Amber–Green status. If you know you cannot hit one, you will need to formally re-baseline the schedule. We'll talk more about this in Chapter 7, but for now, the main principle is that the milestones are the high-level, key dates that you, your Sponsor and other key stakeholders will use to track adherence to the schedule. But they also give you the freedom to manage *all the other tasks in the schedule* as you see fit. That's quite empowering – let's have a look at how it's done.

MANAGING – AND ADAPTING – THE PLAN

It is important to note that no project plan that I have ever put together looked the same at the end of the project as it did at the beginning (though most of the key milestones and end dates would have remained the same). It is a common misconception that the plan is something that is to be encased in glass and rigidly stuck to. This is simply not the case. Anyone who has ever attempted to construct even the most high-level plan will know that most plans are out of date before you are able to press "print."

The fact is the plan should be reviewed and updated regularly. Tasks will move around, and some will take slightly longer to deliver than planned, some slightly shorter. But the plan must change under control. Whenever you sit down (with the project team) and review the plan, you must create an environment where people feel comfortable telling you if a task is running late, or has run into difficulties. The alternative is that they don't tell you and you find out too late. Early notification of issues means they can be resolved, or at the very least mitigated.

But – and it's an important but – at the same time, you must constructively challenge why a task is not delivering to the originally planned timescale. If a task is genuinely running late, you and your team need to be thinking about the following (in roughly increasing order of magnitude from minor correction to major re-plan):

- Is there any float on that activity? Can the delay be accommodated without any impact to any other part of the plan?

- What can be done to recover the time so that the overall plan remains on track? For example, can a subsequent task be done more quickly to compensate?
- Are any other tasks affected by this delay? What can be done to recover *that* time?
- Is there something creative we can do to get the task back on track?
- Are any milestones affected by the delay?
- Can we use any of our planning contingency to soak up the impact?*
- Is there an underlying planning assumption that is at fault (e.g. have we been too optimistic in our estimates of how long things will take)? If so, what other tasks might be affected by that assumption – how much of the plan is at risk?

In other words, you should only allow the plan to change once you have fully considered why a task is delayed and considered all the options for keeping your milestones protected and the *overall* plan on track.

In truth, I don't get too excited if tasks move around a bit; it's to be expected. There's always some give-and-take once a plan comes off the page and starts to be delivered in the real world. But you should treat the milestones as sacrosanct. Any movement which even looks like it *might* affect a milestone, should be heavily resisted and everyone's brains brought to bear on the challenge of how to manage the plan so that the milestones remain unchanged.

An important point to note here is that if the plan is updated regularly, make sure you have a way to ensure everyone is working to the same version. If the plan gets updated, circulate the latest version to everyone and ensure out-of-date versions are either archived or destroyed. A big risk to any project is that of people working off different versions of the plan. Perhaps have a single location (physical or online) where everyone must go if they want to see the latest plan. The point here is that there must be a single, consistent version of the truth.

On every project I find that there are one or two documents I keep with me that tend to get pulled out regularly. It might be a diagram that neatly summarizes how a particular solution will work, or a communications plan, or a RACI matrix. More often than not though, it will be some representation of the schedule. Perhaps a high-level timeline, a list of

---

* Use this wisely. Before you know it, your planning contingency will be gone.

the key milestones, or even the plan itself to a level of detail where it can be folded and put in my pocket, ready to be whipped out and looked at whenever the need arises.

The schedule is ultimately what will drive your project delivery. Hopefully, you will have found plenty in the preceding pages to help you pull together a schedule you can be proud of. Review it regularly, keep it up-to-date protect your milestones, and you are well on your way to delivering your project successfully.

THE EVERYDAY PROJECT MANAGER SHOULD...

- Plan tasks and sequences forward from a start date, not backward from an end date (wherever possible).
- Plan to the right level of detail – don't get lost in the weeds.
- Ensure every task has an agreed owner.
- Use planning horizons (it's better to be broadly right than precisely wrong).
- Identify your pitons and firebreaks – ensure you have break-points that you can fall back to.
- Baseline your plan and then update it regularly. Ensure it adapts to changes as they occur, but do not allow tasks to slip unchallenged.

6

How Much?!: Budgeting and Cost Management

TRACKING AND MANAGING COSTS

As we know, your job as project manager is to look after the time, cost, and quality elements of the project. The last chapter looked at the schedule, which is where you manage the time element. Now we will look at cost management. There are three parts to cost management on a project. The first part is to work out your budget – that is the amount of money that you believe you will require in order to do the job. The second part is tracking and monitoring your *actual* spend to ensure that you are not exceeding your budget (or identify where you are exceeding your budget so you can plan to bring things back on track). And the final part is cost forecasting, which entails working out – at any point in the project – how much money you will need to finish the project (and when you are likely to need it).

Fortunately, all three elements of cost management – budgeting, tracking, and forecasting – can all be done using a single tool – the project cost plan.

PUT IT ALL INTO A COST PLAN

It doesn't matter if you have a fully qualified project accountant or a cigarette-packet estimate: just make sure you have a cost plan. And, actually, you've done a lot of the work already. Because you've already figured out your objectives and your scope – now you just need to put a cost against them.

The words "cost plan" can strike fear into the hearts of many who think that they are complicated, mysterious things or that you need a degree in accountancy or a doctorate in spreadsheets to be able to use or manage one. In fact, the very best cost plans are pleasingly simple things. Of course, if managing cost is what gets you up in the morning, then you could have a very pretty cost plan in various colors, with all sorts of fancy formulas. But it's not necessary. What is important is that you **have** a cost plan, and that you review it regularly to see how your costs are tracking.* Every cost plan should observe some basic principles though that will help you to keep abreast of how the project money is being spent. I've created hundreds of cost plans over the years, so over the next few pages we'll look at how to build a great cost plan and some principles for cost management that will help you stay on top of your budget.

A GOOD COST PLAN TELLS A STORY

I like to set my cost plans up to tell a story from the left-hand side of the cost plan to the right. As I work across the page from left to right, I should be able to see how the project has developed over time. In order to do this, you start with the original (planned) project budget on the left-hand side. I think of the budget as a snapshot of the starting point for each project – the plan we had when we set out to deliver (**Where We Started**). In the middle you have your spend to date i.e., how much of that original budget has been spent already (**Where We Are Now**). If you deduct what you've spent from your original budget, you are left with whatever we have left to spend. This is the amount that you have left to forecast, so the right-hand side of the plan is a prediction of how the remaining money will be spent until the end of the project (**Where We Are Going**). So from left to right, you have a sort of representation of the past, moving to the present, then looking ahead to the future. Like I say, it tells the story of the project. Here's what a very simple cost plan might look like, to demonstrate these elements and how they fit together (Figure 6.1).

This cost plan is for a four-month road trip to be undertaken by two friends between February and May. At the end of this chapter we'll go

---

* And, as luck would have it, you can find a template cost plan at everydaypm.co.uk/templates that you can tailor to your needs.

Description	ORIGINAL BUDGET	CURRENT STATUS		FORECAST				BUDGET CHECK
	Estimated total cost	Spent so far	Budget remaining	March	April	May	Total	Delta
Gasoline	$ 1,000.00	$ 200.00	$ 800.00	$ 200.00	$ 200.00	$ 250.00	$ 650.00	$ 150.00
Food	$ 1,200.00	$ 448.80	$ 751.20	$ 465.00	$ 450.00	$ 465.00	$ 1,380.00	$ -628.80
Accommodation	$ 3,600.00	$ 685.00	$ 2,915.00	$ 775.00	$ 750.00	$ 775.00	$ 2,300.00	$ 615.00
Insurance	$ 200.00	$ 200.00	$ -	n/a	n/a	n/a	$ -	$ -
Entertainment/sightseeing	$ 4,000.00	$ 945.60	$ 3,054.40	$ 800.00	$ 800.00	$ 1,400.00	$ 3,000.00	$ 54.40
TOTALS	$ 10,000.00	$ 2,479.40	$ 7,520.60	$ 2,240.00	$ 2,200.00	$ 2,890.00	$ 7,330.00	$ 190.60

FIGURE 6.1
Road trip cost plan.

through a worked example of how the cost plan above was arrived at and how it gets managed. For now, let's start at the left-hand side and look at how you estimate your budget.

BUILDING YOUR BUDGET

To build the cost plan we start on the left of the page and begin by estimating our budget – the amount of money we think we will need to deliver everything that needs to be delivered.

A very straightforward way to build up your cost plan, or a sensible health-check that your plan is robust, is to build it in line with your schedule. Within your schedule you will have started by listing out all the activities that need to be done, and who needs to do them – you might even have included certain payment milestones. Well, then you've already done much of the hard work for your cost plan. Grab that list of activities and assign costs to each. Here's an example of how a project schedule can be converted into a cost plan. We're going to go from a high-level schedule, to a high-level cost plan (to give an idea of the rough cost) to a detailed cost plan, where the costs are bottomed out fully. In this case, the project is a professional theater production.* We start with the high-level schedule of activities. Tasks are on the left and we've estimated how long each one will take and when we expect it to happen (Figure 6.2).

As we can see, all the major, expected activities are covered, along with who will be involved and a couple of milestones (Opening Night and Closing Night). The next thing we want to do is to create our initial cost plan, which gives a first estimate of the cost per activity (and therefore of the overall cost). This is sometimes referred to as a Rough Order of Magnitude or ROM cost. All we need to do is assign a cost to each of the bars in our schedule (Figure 6.3).

By assigning a cost (even a "wet finger in the air" cost) to each activity, we very quickly start to build our cost plan. In total, we've had to make 11 educated guesses as to the cost of each activity – not a huge amount of

---

* It is perhaps worth noting that I have never put on a professional theater production, so the costs are not intended to represent the real-life costs of doing so. They are merely there to demonstrate the cost planning principles at work here. Apologies to anyone whose salary I have inadvertently over- or under-inflated.

ID	Task	Who?	April	May	June	July	August	September
1	Review scripts and decide on production	Producer	▮					
2	Assemble production team	Producer		▮				
3	Production design (set, lighting, sound)	Director; set, lighting and sound designers		▮				
4	Auditions and casting	Casting director		▮				
5	Rehearsal period 1 (off stage)	Director, cast			▮	▮	▮	
6	Build set (buy materials, assemble)	Set construction team				▮	▮	
7	Create publicity materials	Designer; producer; marketing team			▮	▮		
8	Marketing campaign	Marketing team				▮	▮	▮
9	Box office open	Theatre manager					▮	▮
10	Rehearsal period 2 (on stage)	Director, cast, backstage team					◇	
11	Opening night	ALL						◇
12	Performances	ALL						▮
13	Closing night	ALL						◇
14	Set strike	Backstage team						▮

FIGURE 6.2

Theater production – high-level schedule.

ID	Task	Who?	April	May	June	July	August	September		TOTAL
1	Review scripts and decide on production	Producer	$1,000						$	1,000.00
2	Assemble production team	Producer	$10,000						$	10,000.00
3	Production design (set, lighting, sound)	Director; set, lighting and sound designers		$8,000					$	8,000.00
4	Auditions and casting	Casting director		$5,000					$	5,000.00
5	Rehearsal period 1 (off stage)	Director, cast				$250,000			$	250,000.00
6	Build set (buy materials, assemble)	Set construction team					$10,000		$	10,000.00
7	Create publicity materials	Designer; producer; marketing team			$8,000				$	8,000.00
8	Marketing campaign	Marketing team					$20,000		$	20,000.00
9	Box office open	Theatre manager					Provided by theatre. No cost to project.			N/A
10	Rehearsal period 2 (on stage)	Director, cast, backstage team					◆		$	30,000.00
11	Opening night	ALL								N/A
12	Performances	ALL						$150,000	$	150,000.00
13	Closing night	ALL						◆		N/A
14	Set strike	Backstage team							$	1,000.00
			$ 5,000.00	$ 21,000.00	$ 66,000.00	$ 135,000.00	$ 138,000.00	$ 128,000.00	$	443,000.00

FIGURE 6.3

Cost-loaded schedule.

work, but we're already getting a good sense of our total cost (about half a million dollars). A couple of things to observe here:

- This is a really handy exercise when you're trying to work out whether the benefits of a project (or at least the cost-related benefits) will be met. Provided we believe the box office takings will exceed $493,000, we can be reasonably sure that we will break even.
- This is the first step in understanding our monthly cost forecast. As well as assigning a cost for each horizontal line to make up our total, we've also taken a vertical slice for each month and (again, using a rough estimate for each task) worked out how much we'll need to spend each month.*

The next step is to convert this into the detailed cost plan. At this point we depart from the schedule somewhat and focus more on the cost. For each of the 14 identified tasks, we'll now go through and start working up the detail. For every one of the headline tasks we now figure out what are the things relating to that task that will cost us money. You will notice that the "Gantt" bars are gone from this example – we're moving out of scheduling and into cost management (Figure 6.4).

This is a really informative stage as you start to put "actual" anticipated cost against the individual activities.† You'll find that certain elements cost far more than you anticipated (the total cost for tasks 1 and 2 have almost doubled) while others are less than you originally thought (task 5 is *much* cheaper). Hopefully, these things balance each other out, and you arrive at an overall cost which is broadly in line with expectations, while the line items have moved around a fair bit. In some cases, you will find that the cost is far greater than you originally anticipated. Now is the time for a conversation with your Sponsor about the effect this might have on the benefits case. Is there a different approach we need to take, or an element of scope that we need to drop to bring the costs back in line with budget expectations?

Finally, if we look to the bottom of the cost plan, we can now sum up each of the columns to arrive at our initial monthly cost forecast (Figure 6.5).

---

* Depending on the size and length of your project, you may not need to go to the level of monthly cost estimates, but for the vast majority of projects, having a monthly sense of your spend is hugely beneficial. It's an indicator of whether (or not) you're staying on track, and it helps you to manage your cashflow – if it's your own money you're spending, that becomes pretty important!

† For layout reasons, I've cropped the plan shown here. If you would like to see the fully worked example, go to everydaypm.co.uk/templates.

ID	Activity	Cost/activity	April	May	June	July	August	September	TOTAL
1	Review scripts and decide on production	$ 2,400.00							
1.1	Producer salary (pro-rata)		$ 2,400.00						$ 2,400.00
2	Assemble production team	$ 16,600.00							
2.1	Producer salary (pro-rata)		$ 2,400.00	$ 2,400.00					$ 4,800.00
2.2	Director salary		$ 2,000.00	$ 2,000.00					$ 4,000.00
2.3	Set designer salary		$ 800.00	$ 1,600.00					$ 2,400.00
2.4	Lighting designer salary		$ 700.00	$ 1,400.00					$ 2,100.00
2.5	Costume designer salary		$ 500.00	$ 1,000.00					$ 1,500.00
2.6	Sound designer salary		$ 600.00	$ 1,200.00					$ 1,800.00
3	Production design (set, lighting, sound)	$ 6,200.00							
3.1	Director salary (pro-rata for this activity)			$ 1,000.00					$ 1,000.00
3.2	Set designer salary			$ 1,600.00					$ 1,600.00
3.3	Lighting designer salary			$ 1,400.00					$ 1,400.00
3.4	Costume designer salary			$ 1,000.00					$ 1,000.00
3.5	Sound designer salary			$ 1,200.00					$ 1,200.00
4	Auditions and casting	$ 8,800.00							
4.1	Casting director (fixed fee)			$ 5,000.00					$ 5,000.00
4.2	Director salary (pro-rata for this activity)			$ 2,000.00					$ 2,000.00
4.3	Producer salary (pro-rata for this activity)			$ 1,800.00					$ 1,800.00
5	Rehearsal period 1 (off stage)	$ 166,000.00							
5.1	Rehearsal space hire				$ 1,500.00	$ 3,000.00	$ 1,500.00		$ 6,000.00
5.2	Director salary (pro-rata for this activity)				$ 5,000.00	$ 10,000.00	$ 5,000.00		$ 20,000.00
5.3	Cast wage bill				$ 30,000.00	$ 60,000.00	$ 30,000.00		$ 120,000.00
5.4	Cast per diems				$ 5,000.00	$ 10,000.00	$ 5,000.00		$ 20,000.00
6	Build set (buy materials, assemble)	$ 9,250.00							
6.1	Materials					$ 3,500.00			$ 3,500.00
6.2	Labour					$ 2,500.00	$ 2,500.00		$ 5,000.00
6.3	Storage						$ 750.00		$ 750.00
7	Create publicity materials	$ 7,200.00							
7.1	Design			$ 2,300.00					$ 2,300.00
7.2	Printing				$ 4,900.00				$ 4,900.00

FIGURE 6.4

Theater cost plan.

ID	Activity	Cost/activity	April	May	June	July	August	September	TOTAL
	TOTALS:	$ 337,050.00	$ 9,400.00	$ 26,900.00	$ 46,400.00	$ 95,750.00	$ 77,700.00	$ 80,900.00	$ 337,050.00

FIGURE 6.5
Monthly forecast.

LINKING COST AND SCHEDULE

It's worth pausing here and just noting the relationship between cost and schedule. Perhaps you've been taking it on faith up until now when I say that time, cost, and quality are intrinsically linked. But here is a real illustration of how, in the project world, cost and schedule are (and should be) completely integrated with one another. The activity list down the left-hand side is what gives us our scope which must be delivered to a certain level of quality which in turn defines how much it will cost and how long it will take. Time affects cost affects quality affects time.

INCLUDING CONTINGENCY AND RISK IN YOUR BUDGET

So far we have looked at what we think it will actually cost to undertake each of the tasks, but we haven't made an allowance for anything to go wrong, or for the cost of an individual line item to come in higher than we were expecting. The final consideration when creating your budget is to make an allowance for contingency and risk – these will be your Get Out of Jail Free cards when things get tricky. In fact, so important are they that it's worth looking into them in a little more detail. Let's start by defining what we mean by contingency and risk, as they are often confused, or taken to mean the same thing – but they should be treated quite differently. Here's why.

CONTINGENCY VERSUS RISK

Contingency is an amount of money that you allow "on top" in case something turns out to be a bit more expensive than you expected. This might be an individual item that you are purchasing, or the project as a whole. Both may have a level of contingency applied. For example, imagine someone is laying a new patio for me as part of my project to landscape my backyard. They tell me the work will take three days and the labor will be

$300/day. I think they are being optimistic, but accept the estimated cost of $900 for three days. However, I might privately allow an extra day in the budget as contingency in case the work over-runs, so I budget for the work to cost $1,200. If the work does now over-run it's less of a problem as I have budgeted for that to happen. Obviously, this approach means you need more money in your budget up-front than you may actually need to deliver the project. You should therefore select the items very carefully that you want to apply contingency to, so that you don't end up with a hugely inflated budget for a job that simply will not cost that much. You should also avoid adding contingency to things like materials where the cost is known and unlikely to change.

Alternatively, you could apply contingency to the project as a whole. Using the landscaping example, let's say the total estimated cost for the project is coming out at $12,500. I might decide to keep the patio cost at the $900 quoted but apply, say, a 10% contingency to the overall budget. So I budget $13,750 for the project overall ($12,500 plus a 10% contingency of $1,250). I now have $1,250 of which I could use $300 if the patio laying runs over by a day, or keep it in the contingency "pot" if it doesn't, to be used if something else over-runs or handed back as underspend at the end of the project.

The amount of contingency you apply should depend on the level of confidence you have in your estimates for the individual line items. If your budget is made up predominantly of items that are of a fixed cost (in other words, your outgoings are going to be fairly predictable), then you will not need a lot of contingency. If your budget is made up of items whose final price is unpredictable (for example, people costs which will go up if the job takes longer than estimated, but may come down if they manage to do the job quicker), then it is sensible to apply more contingency. As a rule of thumb (and in the absence of any other information) between 5% and 10% is a reasonable amount of contingency to include for cost over-runs on most projects, rising to 20% if you think you have a number of "unpredictable" items in your cost plan. The less certainty you have, the more contingency you should build into your budget.*

---

* It is not unreasonable – and I have seen it happen – for a project manager to allow up to 50% of the project cost as contingency when pressed to estimate the project budget on minimal information. This is fine as an opening bid, but you should then seek to reduce the amount of contingency you are holding as cost certainty increases.

Risk works similarly to contingency, which is why the two get confused. However, whilst *contingency* is used to manage uncertainty in relation to individual **items**, *risk* is used to manage uncertainty in relation to **events** that might damage the project. To illustrate the difference, let's imagine that the cement you are using to lay the patio requires eight hours to dry, during which time it cannot rain or it will not set properly. If it doesn't set properly the whole lot needs to be stripped out and the job started again. Now, the cost of cement will be stable, so in your cost plan you do not need to apply contingency to the amount you have budgeted for the "cement" line item. Let's say the cost of the cement is $1,200 to cover the area of the patio. In your cost plan, therefore, you have a section for materials, and a line for cement with $1,200 budgeted. However, in the unlikely event that it rains during the eight-hour window that the cement is setting the cost to your project will increase by:

- $300 – for a day's labor to strip out the badly set cement.
- $1,200 – to buy new cement.
- $300 – for a day's labor to re-lay the new cement over the patio.
- **$1,800 – total cost!**

Being a sensible project manager you are undertaking this outdoor job in the summer, so the chances of rain are fairly small (especially in a single eight-hour window), but not impossible. Clearly, it would not make sense to budget to do the job twice when you only *really* expect to do it once. How do we resolve the need to budget sensibly but also be prepared for unlikely, but foreseeable events? The answer is with a risk budget (as opposed to contingency) that allows for the fact that these are events and therefore each individual event will have an associated *probability* of occurring. In terms of budgeting, you can approach this in one of two ways. One involves a bit more effort, but is more robust – the other involves less effort, but may see you setting aside more money than you need to.

1. More effort: calculate a *probabilized* estimate for each risk event in your plan. To do this, each risk event that you identify has an associated probability assigned and you adjust the budget set aside according to the *likelihood* of that event occurring. If we estimate the chances of rain during the cement-setting window to be 5%, multiply your cost impact by 5% to get a risk budget of $90 ($1,800 × 5% =

$90). There is no sense in keeping $1,800 aside for something you estimate has only a 5% chance of happening. However, if it doesn't happen, you aren't going to be able to cover your $1,800 cost with a mere $90. The way this works, then, is that you must spend time identifying *all* the risks you think might occur and for each of them go through the exercise of estimating total cost if it were to occur as well as the probability. You then add up all the probabilized costs for each risk in your list and that is the risk budget that you set aside. The idea is that, provided your list is reasonably exhaustive, you will have set aside a reasonable amount of money to cover (or at least mostly cover) any single risk event happening, and, because you have estimated the probability of each risk, it is weighted appropriately. Under this model you might end up with a total risk pot of, for argument's sake, $900. This won't be enough to cover your $1,800 risk event, but that's really unlikely to occur anyway, so you take an additional risk that if it does occur you have to find the extra $900. But you're not tying that money up in the meantime on the off-chance a freak event occurs.

2. Less effort: pick a number that you think will cover you and stick it in your risk budget. Much easier – and the recommended approach for The Everyday Project Manager. If you want to be a bit more scientific about it, you could choose what you believe to be your biggest risk, estimate how much it would cost you, and set that amount aside as your risk budget. That way, any single risk that occurs can be paid for out of the risk pot. However, there are a couple of caveats to this approach. First, bear in mind that any single risk can be covered but not all of them, so don't be lulled into a false sense of security – because this approach allows for any individual risk to be covered, there is a tendency to think you will be alright in any event. But it only takes two risk events to occur and you could find yourself in trouble. Second, by not analyzing the individual risks, you may be setting aside more cash than is really necessary. Whether it's your own money or your company's money, you are tying up funds that might be better used elsewhere. Let's say the cement issue ends up being your biggest risk in terms of financial impact, so you set aside $1,800 as your risk budget. That is *twice as much* as if you had used the probability-based approach above, so you might be locking up a lot of money unnecessarily for events that are quite unlikely to occur.

Whichever approach you use, it is sensible to have a line for risk in your project plan so that you can deal with unexpected events.

Above all, you need to keep a mental separation between contingency and risk. Contingency is the amount you inflate by to deal with *individual cost items, or the project as a whole* costing more. Risk is the amount you set aside to deal with *uncertain events* to prevent your project being derailed by matters beyond your control, regardless of whether or not they are foreseeable.*

THE PURPOSE OF THE COST PLAN IS NOT TO CATER FOR EVERY EVENTUALITY

Finally, bear in mind the purpose of the cost plan is **not** to set aside enough money to deal with every possible eventuality that might befall us. The purpose of a cost plan is to budget for the things we absolutely must have and then to have a reasonable amount set aside so that we can deal with all but the most improbable events without having to stop the project and find more money, or re-plan. The cost plan should include only the things you actually believe the project will need to pay for, plus a proportionate contingency and risk budget to get you out of trouble and keep the ship sailing.

SACRIFICING CONTINGENCY AND RISK

Budgeting for contingency and risk is entirely sensible, but both will lock up funds that might never be used, or be better used elsewhere. As part of your regular cost plan reviews, consider whether you are carrying too much contingency or risk in your plan. The closer you get to project completion, the more certain your costs should be, and therefore the less "fat" there should be in your cost plan. This is particularly true of risk for the reason that risks don't just reduce over the life of the project, but actually expire. If you think of the cement example above, once the cement

---

* We've spoken here about risk in relation to cost. For a more detailed insight into risk see Chapter 9.

has set properly, you no longer have the risk that the work needs to be re-done. Depending on which method you used to calculate risk, that is somewhere between $90 and $1,800 that can be freed up and returned. Don't wait until the end of your project to hand back money that you no longer need – it can usually be put to much better use elsewhere.

GO BACK TO THE OBJECTIVES

Before finalizing your cost plan (and, in particular, your budget), it is worth going back to the project objectives* as a final sense-check. Does every item that you are setting aside money for actually contribute to delivering the objectives? If not, why is it on your cost plan? Do the objectives need to be tweaked, or does the cost plan?

ROAD TRIP! A WORKED EXAMPLE OF A COST PLAN

Earlier in the chapter we had a quick look at an example cost plan for a road trip. Using this simplified example, let's walk through how the budget was estimated† and how the cost plan now gets managed (Figure 6.6).

This cost plan is for a four-month road trip to be undertaken by two friends, Madeleine and Harrison, between February and May. They have managed to save $5,000 each so have a $10,000 budget.

They now need to estimate how much they will need for each of the budget items. Over the four months, they estimate they will need:

- $250/month for gas ($1,000).
- 120 days' worth of food at $10/day ($1,200).
- 120 days' worth of accommodation at $30/day ($3,600).
- $200 for insurance. One-off payment before the start of the trip.

---

* I know, I'm a broken record.
† The purpose of this example is to demonstrate the mechanics of a cost plan, so I have really simplified the scenario. In practice, if you were planning a road trip like this, you would probably have more than five budget items, and the estimates would probably have a bit more science behind them. But you get the idea.

	ORIGINAL BUDGET	CURRENT STATUS			FORECAST				BUDGET CHECK
Description	Estimated total cost	Spent so far	Budget remaining	March	April	May	Total		Delta
Gasoline	$ 1,000.00	$ 200.00	$ 800.00	$ 200.00	$ 200.00	$ 250.00	$ 650.00		$ 150.00
Food	$ 1,200.00	$ 448.80	$ 751.20	$ 465.00	$ 450.00	$ 465.00	$ 1,380.00		$ -628.80
Accommodation	$ 3,600.00	$ 685.00	$ 2,915.00	$ 775.00	$ 750.00	$ 775.00	$ 2,300.00		$ 615.00
Insurance	$ 200.00	$ 200.00	$ -	n/a	n/a	n/a	$ -		$ -
Entertainment/sightseeing	$ 4,000.00	$ 945.60	$ 3,054.40	$ 800.00	$ 800.00	$ 1,400.00	$ 3,000.00		$ 54.40
TOTALS	$ 10,000.00	$ 2,479.40	$ 7,520.60	$ 2,240.00	$ 2,200.00	$ 2,890.00	$ 7,330.00		$ 190.60

FIGURE 6.6
Road trip cost plan.

These are high-level estimates, but they're not trying to plan every last move – it's a road trip so they want to keep things a bit flexible. That takes them to $6,000, so the remaining $4,000 is what they have left for sightseeing during the day and entertainment in the evenings. They have a couple of things they definitely want to do and see along the way, so there are a couple of known costs, and they reckon $1,000/month should be enough to cover those and anything else they might want to do. They write down their estimates in column A of the cost plan and that's their budget figured out. If they are not going to run out of money, they must try not to exceed any of these estimates, or they will need to adjust their plan (Figure 6.7).

At the end of February, they decide to take stock and see how they are doing against their original budget. They add a column (B) and write down how much they have actually spent against each of their budget lines (Figure 6.8).

Having estimated a monthly cost of $250, they ended up putting gas in the tank once a week, each time topping up $50 worth, so they only ended up spending $200 in February. They've covered the amount of ground they had hoped to cover, and plan to cover similar distances over the next couple of months, so maybe the $250/month estimate was a bit high. Good – we can revise that estimate down for the remaining months and we might be able to make a bit of a saving.

But wait – oh, no. It turns out the $10/day estimate for food was *seriously* undercooked. In 28 days they've spent a little under $450. They haven't

Description	A ORIGINAL BUDGET Estimated total cost
Gasoline	$ 1,000.00
Food	$ 1,200.00
Accommodation	$ 3,600.00
Insurance	$ 200.00
Entertainment/sightseeing	$ 4,000.00
TOTALS	$ 10,000.00

FIGURE 6.7
Initial budget.

	A	B
	ORIGINAL BUDGET	**CURRENT STATUS**
Description	**Estimated total cost**	**Spent so far**
Gasoline	$ 1,000.00	$ 200.00
Food	$ 1,200.00	$ 448.80
Accommodation	$ 3,600.00	$ 685.00
Insurance	$ 200.00	$ 200.00
Entertainment/sightseeing	$ 4,000.00	$ 945.60
TOTALS	$ 10,000.00	$ 2,479.40

FIGURE 6.8
Budget and spend to date.

been eating extravagantly – it turns out food was just more expensive than they had allowed for. They'll need to adjust that estimate up considerably – wiping out the saving they'd made on gas.

Let's skip through the others: despite a couple of pricy stopovers, accommodation has, on the whole, been cheaper than anticipated and they've learned the sort of place to go for now that offers a decent room at a fair price. The insurance was paid before the start of the trip so that $200 is done, but no further cost is expected there. Finally, they are just under their estimate for entertainment and sightseeing, but they want to hold some money back for a couple of expensive items in May, so they decide to have a few rest days in March and April to stay on budget.

If we deduct column B from column A, we can see how much money we have left to spend on each item in column C (Figure 6.9).

Now to forecast our remaining spend. There are two ways you could do that from here. You could take the amount you have remaining (column C)

	A	B	C
	ORIGINAL BUDGET	**CURRENT STATUS**	
Description	**Estimated total cost**	**Spent so far**	**Budget remaining**
Gasoline	$ 1,000.00	$ 200.00	$ 800.00
Food	$ 1,200.00	$ 448.80	$ 751.20
Accommodation	$ 3,600.00	$ 685.00	$ 2,915.00
Insurance	$ 200.00	$ 200.00	$ -
Entertainment/sightseeing	$ 4,000.00	$ 945.60	$ 3,054.40
TOTALS	$ 10,000.00	$ 2,479.40	$ 7,520.60

FIGURE 6.9
Budget remaining.

and try to apportion it across the time that you have remaining. Let's take our food budget. Of our original budget we have $750 and change to last three months. So it seems logical to say that we now forecast $250/month in March, April, and May, and try very hard not to exceed that. While this is a perfectly valid approach, you can maybe see the issue it causes. We've already said that our road-trip duo have not eaten out extravagantly – they just misjudged their original estimate. Realistically, they don't stand a chance of keeping to $250/month for the next three months when they've just spent $450 in one month without being particularly excessive.

I would suggest therefore that it is better to learn from our real-life experience of the last month, as that's the best indicator of what will happen over the next three. We should forecast in each month what we *actually think we're going to spend*. That is what a forecast is, after all. Good cost – and project – management is about being honest about the issues and working out what to do about them. It should not be about setting unrealistic boundaries that become a millstone around our necks and make it nigh-on impossible to achieve success.

So – the updated monthly forecast now looks like Figure 6.10.

Here's what we did:

- We reckon we'll spend the same on gas in March and April as we did in February as we're covering similar distances, so $200 in each. In May we have a little further to go so we'll allow an extra $50 top-up, making May's estimate $250.
- Our $10/day estimate for food has turned out to be closer to $15/day so we refine our estimate. $15 × 31 days in March = $465; 30 days in April = $450; and 31 in May = $465.
- In the same way, our $30/day for accommodation gets revised down to a more realistic $25/day.
- The insurance was a one-off payment, so it's not applicable in the forecast.
- We need to hold some money back for a couple of expensive activities we have planned in the final month. But we did something every day in February, so by having a few planned quiet days in March and April we can reduce our expected outgoings for entertainment and still cover the cost of the more expensive activities in May.
- Last, but not least, we add up our forecast to see how much we are forecasting to spend for the remainder of the trip (column D).

Description	ORIGINAL BUDGET	CURRENT STATUS		FORECAST			
	Estimated total cost (A)	Spent so far (B)	Budget remaining (C)	March	April	May	Total (D)
Gasoline	$ 1,000.00	$ 200.00	$ 800.00	$ 200.00	$ 200.00	$ 250.00	$ 650.00
Food	$ 1,200.00	$ 448.80	$ 751.20	$ 465.00	$ 450.00	$ 465.00	$ 1,380.00
Accommodation	$ 3,600.00	$ 685.00	$ 2,915.00	$ 775.00	$ 750.00	$ 775.00	$ 2,300.00
Insurance	$ 200.00	$ 200.00	$ -	n/a	n/a	n/a	$ -
Entertainment/sightseeing	$ 4,000.00	$ 945.60	$ 3,054.40	$ 800.00	$ 800.00	$ 1,400.00	$ 3,000.00
TOTALS	$ 10,000.00	$ 2,479.40	$ 7,520.60	$ 2,240.00	$ 2,200.00	$ 2,890.00	$ 7,330.00

FIGURE 6.10
Budget, spend, and forecast.

Let's add one more column which deducts the remaining spend that we are forecasting (column D) from our remaining budget (column C) to give us a view on our underspend/overspend (column E) (Figure 6.11).

A positive number in column E is underspend (i.e., money to spare), a negative number is overspend (our budget shortfall).

This gives us our complete cost plan for the end of February. Good job.

Now we can do a little analysis. Our shortfall on food means we are overspending our budget by nearly $630, but this is almost completely canceled out by our underspend on accommodation ($615). Overall, we are forecasting that we should come in just $190.60 under our $10,000 budget.

A good cost plan will regularly refine the forecast to match the events that take place in the real world – as we have done here. It allows us to see how money has been spent and use that information to adjust our plan for the future – re-forecasting regularly so we can update our stakeholders, especially of course, our Sponsor, who will usually be paying for all this.

This example has two final things to highlight. The first: I can hear some readers saying "How convenient: you create an imaginary cost plan for a made-up scenario and when it's all worked through it happens to come in under budget. What if it hadn't?" Hmm. Fair point. Let's take a look at that in a moment.

The second thing to highlight is about baselines. A budget can be baselined at a number of levels. If you're the Sponsor, you might say "I have $10,000 to achieve these objectives in six months. I don't care how it's done, or how that money is managed in the intervening period. Just come back in six months with the job done and without exceeding the budget." In this case, you are baselining the *total* project cost. The road-trip scenario above is likely to fall into this category. Two friends have saved $10,000 for a road-trip. As long as they get from A to B and get to do a few key activities along the way, they probably won't be too worried that they spend slightly more on food, but less on accommodation. As long as the *total* remained within budget, all is good. Individual line items can exceed their budgets, provided the overspend is matched by a shortfall elsewhere.

Let's imagine though, that their parents have agreed to pay for the gas. Now it doesn't matter what happens to the overall budget: they have an individual line item that cannot exceed its budget. Similarly, as Sponsor, if you wanted to exert a little more financial control you might say "The

Description	ORIGINAL BUDGET Estimated total cost	CURRENT STATUS Spent so far	Budget remaining	FORECAST March	April	May	Total	BUDGET CHECK Delta
Gasoline	$ 1,000.00	$ 200.00	$ 800.00	$ 200.00	$ 200.00	$ 250.00	$ 650.00	$ 150.00
Food	$ 1,200.00	$ 448.80	$ 751.20	$ 465.00	$ 450.00	$ 465.00	$ 1,380.00	$ -628.80
Accommodation	$ 3,600.00	$ 685.00	$ 2,915.00	$ 775.00	$ 750.00	$ 775.00	$ 2,300.00	$ 615.00
Insurance	$ 200.00	$ 200.00	$ -	n/a	n/a	n/a	$ -	$ -
Entertainment/sightseeing	$ 4,000.00	$ 945.60	$ 3,054.40	$ 800.00	$ 800.00	$ 1,400.00	$ 3,000.00	$ 54.40
TOTALS	$ 10,000.00	$ 2,479.40	$ 7,520.60	$ 2,240.00	$ 2,200.00	$ 2,890.00	$ 7,330.00	$ 190.60

FIGURE 6.11

Full road trip cost plan.

project manager is in charge of spending on each line item, but I want to know about the overall project cost **but also** I should be notified if any individual budget line is forecasting an overspend." Similarly to milestones in the schedule, the budget is used as a baseline and it could be done at overall project level, or several levels of detail down from there.

Taking these two points together, let's re-imagine our scenario. In the new scenario, Madeleine wants to go on a road trip. She has recently had a $10,000 windfall and wants to go away. She doesn't know what she wants to do, but her best friend Harrison suggests going on a road trip. Madeleine loves the idea, but hates planning trips, so agrees to pay for it all on the proviso that Harrison plans it all. She doesn't really mind how the money is spent, as long as they don't exceed the $10,000. That said, she does want to be involved in some of the decision-making so she and Harrison agree that if any one item looks like it will be exceeded, Madeleine will be involved in the decision about what to do – and as it's her money, she will have the final say. The project itself is the same as before, but we have baselined at overall budget level and line item level. And this time they ended up spending $75 on each gasoline top-up rather than $50, so we've updated the forecast accordingly.

Figure 6.12. shows how the new plan looks at the end of February with the more expensive gasoline.

In this case, Harrison (the project manager) would have to report that we are forecasting to exceed our gas and food budgets, and as a result the overall project budget is also forecast to be exceeded.* Madeleine (the Sponsor) is then given the ultimate decision about how to manage this, though obviously she will involve her project manager in the discussion. Madeleine might decide that rather than trying to thin down the budget elsewhere, she is prepared to inject a bit more cash from her savings to cover the extra $275 for gasoline, changing the overall project budget from $10,000 to $10,275. Or Harrison might offer to pay the difference out of his savings, opening up another funding source they hadn't considered when the budget was first worked up. Again, the overall project budget changes from $10,000 to $10,275, but the solution has been reached in a different way.

---

* Note: we are *forecasting* to exceed – we haven't exceeded it yet (in fact, we've only spent just over a quarter of the budget). Good project management is about looking ahead and flagging issues before they become issues.

Description	ORIGINAL BUDGET Estimated total cost	CURRENT STATUS Spent so far	Budget remaining	FORECAST March	April	May	Total	BUDGET CHECK Delta
Gasoline	$ 1,000.00	$ 300.00	$ 700.00	$ 300.00	$ 300.00	$ 375.00	$ 975.00	$ -275.00
Food	$ 1,200.00	$ 448.80	$ 751.20	$ 465.00	$ 450.00	$ 465.00	$ 1,380.00	$ -628.80
Accommodation	$ 3,600.00	$ 685.00	$ 2,915.00	$ 775.00	$ 750.00	$ 775.00	$ 2,300.00	$ 615.00
Insurance	$ 200.00	$ 200.00	$ -	n/a	n/a	n/a	$ -	$ -
Entertainment/sightseeing	$ 4,000.00	$ 945.60	$ 3,054.40	$ 800.00	$ 800.00	$ 1,400.00	$ 3,000.00	$ 54.40
TOTALS	$ 10,000.00	$ 2,579.40	$ 7,420.60	$ 2,340.00	$ 2,300.00	$ 3,015.00	$ 7,655.00	$ -234.40

Column labels: Ⓐ Ⓑ Ⓒ Ⓓ Ⓔ

FIGURE 6.12
Road trip overspend.

In any case, the lesson here is that if any budget line, or the overall project budget, is forecast to be exceeded, the Sponsor *must* be told and the project manager and Sponsor enter into a discussion about how to resolve the overspend. And of course, you must come back to the Holy Trinity – time, cost, quality.

In this case, cost has gone up. If additional cash (i.e., re-baselining the budget) isn't an option, we must look to schedule or quality. Do we cut the road-trip short by two weeks, that way saving 14 days' worth of fuel, food, accommodation, and entertainment? That would surely bring us back under the $10,000 mark. Perhaps, though, they have a sky-dive planned on their final day which Madeleine (as Sponsor) is not willing to forego. So now cost *and* schedule are fixed as we need to maintain the timeline (and at least one scope requirement – the sky-dive). But they've been staying in separate rooms in hotels. It's only February – if they are prepared to spend March and April using dormitory accommodation in a hostel, they could significantly reduce their accommodation costs still further. Yes, at the expense of the quality of their accommodation (or overall experience, possibly – who knows though, they might enjoy it).

The lesson, then, is simple. Review costs regularly – and re-forecast so that you get early awareness of any cost issues. This will enable you to keep your Sponsor informed and – together – adjust the plan to reflect a changing reality.

A cost plan may seem a very dry, mathematical tool but what it enables you to do is adapt your situation in the real world. A good cost plan leaps off the page and into the real world, showing you all the opportunities to keep your project on track and – importantly – on budget.

THE EVERYDAY PROJECT MANAGER SHOULD...

- Establish a baseline budget and track it in a cost plan.
- Have a simple cost plan that makes sense to you – and update it regularly.
- Ensure your cost plan is aligned to your schedule.
- Make allowances within your cost plan for contingency and risk, but sacrifice each as you go.

7

Control Mechanisms: Setting Up Your Project Governance

CHANGE UNDER CONTROL VERSUS CONTROLLING CHANGE

One of the key misconceptions with regard to project management is that success comes from sticking rigidly to a plan and bringing as many elements as possible under your control in order that you can reach your goal. But it is impossible to bring everything under your control. You simply cannot control every last event. We must find ways to adapt to changes under control, rather than attempting to control all change.

Control in the project world comes from having mechanisms in place that allow you to adapt quickly and, where possible, advantageously, to any changes that might come your way. As anyone who has attempted to plan anything will testify, events will inevitably occur that will cause you to pause, re-assess, and possibly change your plans. They might also cause you to despair, weep, or scream into a cushion. Obviously we need to avoid the latter group, and the way we do that is through project governance.

Project governance is the term given to the range of mechanisms you put in place to ensure that the project stays on track to deliver the objectives. It is – once again – worth noting that, provided you have thought carefully about your objectives, defined them clearly, and kept them suitably high-level, there will usually be more than one way to achieve them. This is a good thing as it means you will have some flexibility to adapt to change and still achieve your goal. The key thing is to set up governance that allows you to chart a way through the changes in a conscious, deliberate way and not be at the mercy of events.

Do not get me wrong though. I fully understand that if you have built a sensible, detailed plan based on the objectives and have been on track to deliver on time and within budget, it can be a gut-wrenching thing to realize that you have to make adjustments to your plan. Or worse yet, give it a major overhaul. But always remember – the objectives are the aim of the game. By having the right attitude and allowing changes to come into our plan, strictly under control, we keep the endgame in sight and allow ourselves to stay true to the objectives.

It is also true to say that very often the changes that are brought will improve the end-state, or possibly even allow you to get there more quickly or for less money. Change will happen so there is absolutely no point pretending it won't or sticking stubbornly to a plan which looks more ridiculous and out-of-date by the moment. Far better to greet the change head on, make considered, careful adjustments to the plan and be hailed as the terrific project manager you are for adapting as you go, but still delivering what you set out to deliver. Hooray then, for project governance.*

SETTING YOUR BASELINES

The first concept I'll introduce you to in the world of project governance is that of baselines. A baseline is simply an agreement *at a given point in time* about something to do with the project. The baseline is a statement (or several statements) that represent a commitment to certain constraints according to which the project will deliver – unless something happens which renders that baseline unachievable, at which point the project will need to change. In other words, it's a line in the sand that says "until circumstances change beyond our control this is what we commit to doing."

The baseline is agreed between the project manager (on behalf of the project team) and the Sponsor. It is the project manager's commitment to

---

* Said very few people, ever. But they should – good project governance will always save the day when you hit issues.

the Sponsor in terms of key aspects of the delivery, but it is also what the project manager (and Sponsor) will use as a quick way of understanding if everything is under control.

A project that has been well set up will have several baselines. You will have a schedule baseline, a cost baseline, and a scope baseline as a minimum. Which, of course, reference our Holy Trinity of time, cost, and quality. In other words, your baseline is the agreement that says what you will deliver, by when, and for how much.

For the purpose of The Everyday Project Manager, we can arrive at our three main baselines quite simply.

Your key milestones make up your **schedule baseline**. When it comes to agreeing and signing off the baseline, I find it useful to create a milestone plan. This is simply a table of the key milestones plucked from your plan. If you're building a house, your milestone plan might look like Table 7.1.

If you and your Sponsor have agreed these key milestones, they become your baseline dates. If any of these dates is forecast to be exceeded, you must escalate to your Sponsor as a minimum and potentially consider re-baselining via a change control (see below). In any case, you have your schedule baseline.

Your **cost baseline** is your budget. Whatever is in that left-hand column of your cost plan is what you are aiming to deliver against. From a governance point of view though, it is not practical to manage this at the line-item level. Similarly, the overall project cost is often too crude a measure of how we are managing our project costs. I recommend picking a middle path which groups activities together, so you are not baselining at line item level, but nor are you focusing solely on the overall cost. Depending on how your cost plan has come together, you may find that

TABLE 7.1

Schedule baseline for a house-building project

Activity	Date
Foundations complete	Mar-30
Frame complete	May-02
Structure is weathertight	Sep-07
External construction complete	Oct-18
Carpentry/joinery complete	Dec-07
Electrics and plumbing signed-off	Jan-31
House ready for buyers	Mar-06

TABLE 7.2

Cost baseline for a house-building project

Activity	Cost
Land purchase	$80,000
Surveys	$2,000
Design	$15,000
Materials	$70,000
Labor	$118,000
Risk	$38,500
Total	**$323,500**

these groupings become obvious anyway. If you take the house building example above, our cost baseline summary may look something like Table 7.2.

One thing worth noting is that the land purchase is a single line-item cost but it's of sufficient magnitude and importance that it is worth including as a baseline item in its own right. Just because you don't want to baseline every single line item in your cost plan doesn't mean you can't baseline one or two key ones.

We now have a summarized breakdown of cost that is at a sensible level for us to be able to track and report on it. Which just leaves scope.

There are two levels to which you define your **scope baseline**. The first is the scope outline (see Chapter 3 for information on creating the scope outline). This acts as your agreement with the Sponsor about what you are actually going to deliver. The scope outline is normally a written list, so the simplest way to baseline is to send that list to your Sponsor and ask them to confirm their agreement that, if these activities are all undertaken successfully, the project will have delivered its objectives. The next level to baseline is the requirements and this should follow the same process. Once the requirements are defined, send them to your Sponsor and ask them to confirm that if the project delivers according to the requirements, they will be satisfied that the quality criteria for the project have been met.

CHANGE MANAGEMENT AND RE-BASELINING

The important thing to remember is that change is perfectly acceptable, provided it's done consciously and the plan is re-baselined accordingly.

Some people are (justifiably) reluctant to re-baseline, as they see it as a deviation from what was originally agreed. That might be true, but it misses the point. To re-baseline your project is to recognize that something has changed since you last established your agreed baselines, and that you are now making a conscious decision to change the project to accommodate new information. That is not just a sensible thing to do – surely to do anything else would be irresponsible? The alternative would be to plough on trying to deliver an outcome that is no longer fit-for-purpose or deliver against a set of constraints (time/cost/quality) that are no longer realistic.

With well-defined baselines for cost, schedule, and scope, identifying change becomes a much easier task. If you are reviewing and updating your cost plan regularly, you will quickly identify when your forecast exceeds your baseline. If you are reviewing and updating your schedule regularly, you will quickly identify a shift in the plan that means a milestone is now likely to be missed. Similarly, it is worth reviewing the scope and requirements from time to time, and comparing what was signed off to what is actually being done. Are people working on things that aren't defined in the requirements (scope creep)? Or, in the process of building it, has the solution deviated significantly from what was originally agreed? This is scope change.* And sometimes change is really obvious – your Sponsor needs to save money and cuts the project budget by $10,000. The restaurant opening needs to be brought forward by a week to take advantage of a famous critic being in town. New legislation is announced by the government and the website you were about to launch needs to be revised to remove references to the old legislation. However it arises, if the project changes to the extent that one or more of the baselines is no longer achievable, you will need to agree to change the project accordingly and re-baseline according to the new constraints and requirements.

Now, obviously if you are re-baselining once a week, then there should be warning flags going up left, right, and center. If you need to frequently re-baseline that suggests that you have not put the necessary thought into your time, cost, and quality baselines, and perhaps more work needs to

---

* As you can see, identifying scope change can be slightly more challenging than cost and schedule, as scope can be interpreted more subjectively. A date is a date, and a cost is a cost, but when it comes to *describing* what you will get as a result, the water gets a little murkier.

be done agreeing a schedule, a budget, or a stable set of requirements. But don't be afraid to re-baseline if it's the right thing to do. If the goal changes, move the goalposts accordingly.

A good change management process should be simple and easy-to-follow. If it is too complicated, it will not be followed, and change will find its way into your project through other means (remember our old friend scope creep?). So it's important that everyone on the project team is aware of the process and knows how to raise a change. The process then needs to be simple enough to deal with each change quickly and efficiently to minimize the impact to the project. Some people try to create challenging, complex change processes in order to deter people from raising changes in the first place, but I believe this is counterproductive. It is better by far that you have changes raised frequently which are then dealt with quickly through a clear process, than that you have a change process that is so labyrinthine people sit on changes or introduce them via the back door, only for them to derail your project at a later date.

In any event, all change processes should broadly follow the process outlined below:

Capture the change: I recommend keeping a change log (you'll find a wealth of templates online), but it doesn't need to be particularly formal – it just needs to be written down. Describe the change – what is the additional scope that's been identified or requested? Describe it in sufficient detail that the rest of the team can be clear on what's intended and that estimates of the impact can be undertaken.

Assess the impact of the change: having described it, you can now estimate the impact of the change – and you do this in terms of cost, schedule, and scope. A genuine change is something that was not in your original baseline, and therefore it stands to reason that working it into a revised plan will have an impact on either your budget, your schedule, or your scope – or a combination.

For scope changes, it might be that incorporating a new request won't cause the project to delay, but will make it cost a bit more. For example, let's say I've decided that in my new kitchen I want to change the worktops from wood to tile. It takes exactly the same amount of time to install either worktop, but the tile is more expensive. I will need to adjust my budget upwards, but the schedule is unaffected. Alternatively, I might decide I would like a different worktop that costs exactly the same, but is on a lead time that is three weeks longer than the original worktop. My cost baseline remains the same, but the schedule will now extend.*

If the change is to your budget, e.g. we need to save $10,000 on the overall project cost, then the impact will be described in terms of schedule and/ or scope. The solution to a $10,000 budget cut might be to reduce the size of the team on the understanding that the remaining team members will take longer to deliver the project. Alternatively, in order to save the $10,000, you might simply drop an element of scope (e.g. the new kitchen is costing $10,000 more than we had budgeted for, but if we decide to go without the underfloor heating we can deliver it for our original budget; or we identify that large parts could be pre-fabricated rather than bespoke, achieving the cost expectation, but reducing the quality of the final product).

The final permutation is, of course, a schedule change which will have its impact described in terms of cost and/or scope. Let's imagine the Sponsor signed off the original schedule, but a change somewhere else in the business means she now would like to see if the project could be delivered a month earlier. If you outsource one of the tasks to an agency, then you can run that task in parallel, freeing up your project team and enabling you to bring another task in earlier, giving you the extra month needed. But you now need to pay the agency, so the cost goes up. Alternatively, when looking at the scope in conjunction with the schedule you are able to identify two Could-Have requirements on your critical path. By removing them, the project timeline reduces by a month.

It is pertinent to note that, while there are trade-offs, they won't all necessarily be downsides. While you may have to reduce the scope of your project in order to achieve a schedule saving, you will no longer be paying for the scope that you have removed, so as well as saving on time, you are also making a cost saving. Similarly, if you reduce cost by going with pre-fabricated units rather than bespoke, it is highly likely that they can be available more quickly and the schedule reduced accordingly. When we talk about the impact of the change, it is important to capture both the positive and the negative impacts. See the example below.

---

* Bear in mind, it may extend by more than the three-week additional lead time. That three-week delay might mean that other tasks have to be rescheduled, or that the people lined up to do the work become unavailable. If the carpenter lined up to install your worktop has two weeks of work lined up at the point your new worktop is delivered, the three-week delay is now five weeks, as you wait for the carpenter to become available again. Always ensure you are assessing the **full** impact to your project, not just the immediate impact of the change itself.

These first two steps (*capture the change* and *assess the impact of the change*) form the Change Request. In real-world project management a Change Request (sometimes called a Change Control) is a formal document, but that doesn't mean it has to be complicated. In fact, the best performing projects that I've worked on keep it really simple. All the information should fit on a single sheet of paper. An example change request might therefore look something like Figure 7.1.

Different organizations might demand that other information is captured on a Change Request (usually operational information specific to that organization – for example, will a change to a building require an electrical shutdown whilst it is done). The change request template that you use should be flexible to include the specific information required by the organization you are delivering the project for, but should contain **as a minimum** the information detailed above.

When the change request is complete, the next step is to submit it.

Submit the change for a decision: As part of setting up your project's governance, you will need to decide who is empowered to make decisions about various things – including change requests (see also Steering Groups and Terms of Reference, later in the chapter). As the overall accountable owner of the project, the Sponsor should at the very least sign-off on

KITCHEN EXTENSION PROJECT		Requestor:	L. Canfield
Reason for change and brief description			
When looking at the design we realised that if we extend by an extra 3 feet we will be able to accommodate a washing machine within the planned workspace. This would mean the washing machine could be moved from the garage freeing up much-needed storage space and improving the flow of the house.			

Change type	Impact statement
Scope increase	Additional 3-foot extension to western elevation of plan. Moderate re-design required.
Scope reduction	n/a
Schedule	Fully redesigning the space will add an extra week, but it is believed the project end date could be maintained.
Cost	The redesign will cost approx. $800, whilst the additional materials needed to extend will cost in the region of $2,500. Total cost: $3,300.

Schedule					Cost		
Milestone	Baseline	Revised	Variance		Baseline	Change	Revised
Design complete	6th March	13th March	7 days		$32,400	$3,300	$35,700

FIGURE 7.1
Example Change Request.

any change (or be a member of the group that does agree change). On smaller, simpler projects it might be that the Sponsor's approval is the only approval required. In which case, you simply submit the change request to the Sponsor requesting their approval (or not). On larger projects it might fall to a group of people to review changes on a regular basis and agree that they can change (if a group is convened to review changes they are commonly referred to as the Change Board). In any case, it is perhaps worth noting that whoever approves changes must have the authority to do so. It is no good having a member of the management team sign-off on a $10,000 cost increase if they do not actually have the budget or financial authority to make that decision. However, the point is to ensure that there is agreement around which person, or group of people, will meet to review changes. Again, depending on the scale of the project, the formality of this arrangement will vary. In some cases an email from the Sponsor is enough. For a large, expensive, lengthy project linked closely to a firm's strategic objectives it might be that all changes have to go to the Executive Board for approval, with the decision recorded in the minutes of the Board meeting. At all events, establish at the start of the project who will review changes and how frequently. Change requests are submitted to the Change Board for approval. The Change Board will review each change request, or set of change requests, taking account of the full impact of each change. If the impact is deemed to be tolerable, they may approve the change. If not, they may reject it.

Record and re-baseline: Once the Change Board have made their decision, that decision must be recorded (again, keeping a change log will mean you have a single central place to refer to all change-related decisions). If the change is rejected, it is still important to record that the change was submitted, reviewed, and rejected so that everyone is clear on the outcome. If people have spent some time considering the change and its impact, it might be easy for them to assume that this is the new direction, so clear communication of a rejection is just as important as it is for an approval. This also creates an audit trail and prevents any confusion later about whether or not a change was agreed. In the event of rejection, the existing project baselines stand and the project continues to deliver to those baselines as if nothing had changed, because now – officially – nothing *has* changed.

If the change is approved, again this must be recorded, preferably on a central change log. Then all affected baselines must be updated accordingly and various processes will probably be triggered, depending on the organization involved. For example, if the Change Board approves a scope change that has an associated cost impact of $10,000, the project's budget will need to be increased by $10,000, the cost report updated, and the funds released to the project. As part of their impact assessment for a schedule change, the project team will need to have worked up a new version of the project schedule which accounts for the change. This revised schedule becomes the new schedule baseline and everyone needs to start working to this schedule, maybe even removing old schedules from circulation to prevent confusion (I once worked on a project where we had to instruct contractors to destroy copies of outdated schedules after a major issue was caused by people working to different versions of the project schedule). The approved scope or requirements documentation will need to be updated and the new version circulated to all those that require it, so that everyone is clear on the new project specification.

In any case, communication is key (as always). Ensure everyone on the project team is aware of the approval and that all associated baselines are updated and recirculated as appropriate. This is called re-baselining the project, and the new baseline replaces the old one as the official agreement about what the project will deliver.

As you can see, by applying this process, the project might end up delivering something quite different from what was agreed in the *original* baseline documents. But, provided all change has gone through an appropriate change control process, there should be an easily traceable path from the original baseline, through the changes, to the last agreed baseline. As long as the project delivers according to the last agreed baseline, it will still have delivered successfully, even if that baseline is radically different from the original.

TOLERANCES

One way to minimize surprises (and – among other things – project management is about minimizing surprises) is to agree tolerances on your baselines. This provides your Sponsor with an early warning, while giving you a bit of flexibility. The idea is that you agree your baseline, but then add a tolerance in either direction. For example, you might agree a budget of (for simplicity's sake) $1,000 with a 10% tolerance. The Sponsor agrees that if you deliver the project for $1,100 then, hey, we'll still call that "within budget." This is helpful in situations where you have several unknowns at the point you are trying to set your budget. So you set a nominal budget, but allow a tolerance on the basis that it would be unfair to pin you to a figure with several things you cannot yet quantify. In return, you offer up 10% in the other direction to say that when it looks like the costs will exceed $900, you'll put up a flag that the budget may be exceeded.*

Another example of the same concept applied to your schedule could be that you agree to deliver by next April, with a one-month tolerance. In this case, you'll raise a flag if it looks like it's going to be later than March, but we'll still consider things successful if the project delivers in May. This follows the logic of "it is better to be broadly right than precisely wrong" that we discussed in Chapter 5 in relation to planning. By setting tolerances (provided the tolerances are acceptable to all concerned) you are making the criteria for success far easier to achieve, without really giving anything up. Imagine for example that, as a Sponsor, you are happy as long as the project is delivered before July 31st. Ideally you want it done a couple of weeks before the 31st so that you can relax knowing it's done. You could baseline a project end date of July 15th. If the project delivers on the 17th, it is considered to have missed its target, and failed. But you could agree that the project will target delivery against a baseline of July 15th, with a one-week tolerance. In other words, as long as the project delivers within one week of the baseline date (i.e. any time up to July 22nd) you, as Sponsor, will be satisfied that the project has done what is needed. The project that delivered on the 17th would be a success now, rather than a failure; you have sponsored a successful project and still received the outcome well ahead of when you needed it.†

You may also introduce tolerances to prevent change being triggered too frequently. If you have a line item in your cost plan that is estimated to cost $1,000 and in the event costs $1,001.20, I think most people would agree it is perhaps over the top to be setting off flares and invoking a change management process, causing your cost plan to be fully re-baselined. A more reasonable approach might be to agree, say, a 10% tolerance on

---

* Which, of course, as a good project manager, you would do anyway – but this formalizes the arrangement.
† Note that the baseline date does not change. The project should still be targeting and planning in order to hit July 15th. The only thing that's changed is that we've applied a tolerance to that date.

any individual line item along with a 5% tolerance on the overall project budget. For the sake of simplicity, let's say you have 20 line items in your cost plan, each costing $1,000, giving a total project cost of $20,000. You agree the tolerances above with your Sponsor, so any individual line item can be forecast up to $1,100 before you raise the alarm. However, by adding the project-level tolerance we are putting a further tripwire in place, such that only ten items could come in at the upper level of cost. At a 5% tolerance on total project cost, as soon as the project budget is forecast to exceed $21,000, you would raise the alert with your Sponsor.

Similarly, to use the earlier scheduling example, if your project baseline end date is July 15th, and you are forecasting that you will deliver on the 20th, you should be raising a change in order to re-baseline your end date. But if your baseline is July 15th with a one-week tolerance, your forecast date of the 20th is within tolerance and a change is not required (but you will certainly raise one if the forecast extends beyond the 22nd).

As you can see, setting tolerances is a good way to allow yourself some flexibility because life is uncertain, and you don't want to be pushing the panic button every five minutes. At the same time, they allow the Sponsor to use the governance to maintain a level of control without concerning themselves every time the project overspends by a penny, or delays by a day.

GOVERNANCE GATEWAYS

Another method by which governance is used to control projects is by introducing governance gateways. These are break-points inserted into the over-arching project process (so they apply to all projects being delivered in a portfolio). A project gateway is a set of criteria that must be satisfied in order for the project to proceed any further. Normally a project will be required to go to its governing or Steering Group (see later in the chapter for more information on these) in order to request approval to proceed. Typically, the project manager and Sponsor would attend to present the fact that all conditions have been met and request approval from those present. The members of the Steering Group then have the opportunity to ask questions and satisfy themselves that the project has indeed met the necessary criteria and can proceed. Importantly, project gateways are an opportunity to review the project at key stages in its lifecycle and decide if it should be stopped. This might be because, despite work done, the world has moved on, and the objectives are no longer achievable, or the benefits no longer realistic. If that were the case, it would be foolish to continue working on the project – at least in its current guise. This can be hugely disappointing for a project manager and their team who have invested their time, energy, and passion into a project so far – especially if the project has been going for some time already. But it shouldn't be viewed in this way. Stopping projects that are destined to fail is good project governance and prevents further investment of time, money, resources, and energy which will be wasted if the outcomes are either no longer desired or achievable.

Gateways are defined in several ways and, as stated, will typically be set at portfolio-level so all projects being delivered will be subject to them. As a project manager therefore you are unlikely to be involved in the definition of gateways, but you will absolutely need to be aware of any gateways that will apply to your project, as well as the criteria that you must satisfy to pass them.

They will typically be inserted between stages of a project (e.g. between completing design and starting construction) and at points before key commitments (usually financial) are being made. A project process that incorporates gateways might insist that all projects in the portfolio have the gateways shown in Table 7.3, for example.

The gateways therefore act as checks. I like to think of them as lay-bys on the road approaching a major junction. Before you find yourself in the middle of the junction, pull over into the lay-by, check the map to confirm your direction, check that you still have enough fuel in the tank to get there, and that the engine light hasn't come on. Once you're happy everything is in order, get back on the road.

<hr/>

THE PROJECT MANAGEMENT OFFICE (PMO)

In medium-to-large organizations, the work of managing project governance becomes a job in itself and people are employed full-time to look after these control mechanisms.* The business unit that looks after

---

* Honestly, that is how important they are when managing a portfolio of projects.

TABLE 7.3

Example governance gateways

Gateway	Description	Why?
Gateway 1	Requirements sign-off	This ensures that no work is undertaken on designing or constructing a solution until there is a clear, agreed statement of what the project is delivering. This means the project will be setting off on the right footing. It is also common that, up until requirements sign-off, the costs have been minimal, as defining the project does not require a great deal of outside investment.
Gateway 2	Design complete	Once you have a description of your solution (be it an architect's drawing or a 200-page proposal for how a new working practice will be rolled out to a company), it is advisable to stop and check that the solution has taken account of all of the requirements. All should agree that delivery of the proposed solution will indeed represent delivery of the objectives.
Gateway 3	Begin construction	This may follow on quickly from design solution, or maybe you'll have tendered the design out and gone through a procurement process. In any case, before anyone puts a spade in the ground and you commit to the delivery in earnest, it is prudent to pause and have everyone agree that the project should proceed.
Gateway 4	Handover and close	Formal agreement that the project has completed and handed over a solution that meets the scope and requirements. The project can now close.

governance is known as the Project Management Office or PMO, and I cannot even begin to overstate the value that is added to an organization by having a good Project Management Office. Why? Because the PMO monitors and reports on those key tenets of project management: time, cost, and quality. If you are fortunate enough to be working in a project organization that has a good PMO, then I recommend you work closely with them to ensure the governance on your project is functioning appropriately. The work of the PMO is to report on everything we've covered in this chapter at a program- or portfolio-level.* That means they collect time, cost, and quality information† on *all* the projects within a program or portfolio.

---

* For a reminder on the definitions of program and portfolio, see Introduction: Part Two.
† Not to mention risk, as well as a number of other key performance indicators, typically.

At a high level, the role of the PMO is to collect and analyze information in order to produce reports or other materials that allow managers to make decisions. The PMO is also responsible for the standardization of project materials, for example, ensuring that everyone is using the same change request template, so the Change Board does not have to spend time figuring out where to find the relevant information across six different change requests all submitted in a completely different format from one another.

You wouldn't need a PMO for a single project – its function is to provide consistency across a number of projects or programs within a portfolio, so it is perhaps not relevant for the purposes of The Everyday Project Manager, but if you find yourself getting more into project management, you'll come across a PMO sooner or later.

REPORTING

A fundamental part of the governance in larger project organizations is reporting. As with the PMO, you are highly unlikely to need a structured reporting methodology in place for a single small project. However, while you are unlikely to "report" to yourself, reports are a way of keeping track of progress of projects, and particularly how well (or otherwise) they are doing. A report is an opportunity to take stock at a point in time in your project's delivery and see how things are going. So whether you create a formal report or not, the principle below will help give you an insight into how your project is coming along. And if you are working on a project where you're required to report on your progress, it is important to make sure you are reporting on the right things. A report can be an extremely useful tool for a project manager to help give early warning of potential issues or flag where your stakeholders need to be getting involved and drumming up support.

Before you start reporting, you need to know what to report on. If you've dealt with business reporting before you may be familiar with the term key performance indicators – or KPIs. These are the measure by which we judge how well a product or service (or project) is performing. A customer service desk might have KPIs relating to the number of queries they have handled, or a score of customer satisfaction. A car dealership might have

KPIs relating to the number of cars sold, how much repeat business they attract, or how many people also buy their insurance via the dealership. KPIs are therefore a metric, agreed up-front, specific to the service being provided, that give you a measure of how well you are performing. You will be unsurprised to learn then that the main KPIs for the project manager will be related to time, cost, and quality. The KPI in each case is your baseline and you should report on your performance in relation to that baseline. We'll look below at how you report meaningfully against each baseline but before we do, here are a couple of other things to think about when you are reporting your progress.

RAG STATUSES

If you've never heard of a RAG status before, it stands for Red-Amber-Green and provides a really simple, visual way of highlighting progress or drawing attention to issues. In keeping with traffic lights which warn us that red is danger, amber means caution advised, and green is go, RAG statuses give a quick, easy-to-understand summary. For each of the items you are reporting on, you decide whether the status is red, amber, or green depending on **pre-defined** criteria. The last part of that sentence is often overlooked and it can seriously undermine reporting across an organization. You must agree up-front what the criteria are for red, amber, and green statuses being applied. I have worked in several teams and organizations where they take it on trust that people will apply these statuses sensibly, only to end up with highly subjective judgments being made. A risk-averse project manager declares everything red, causing time and energy to be wasted worrying about issues that are not really issues. Or a more gung-ho project manager has a serious issue on their hands, but reports it as green as they are confident they can fix it and don't want people getting stressed about it or asking too many questions. Obviously, neither of these situations is good, so you need to agree what is meant by each status and endeavor to make the criteria as objective as possible. The rule of thumb that I use on most projects is as follows:

- **Green:** everything is on track and we are on course to deliver against our baselines.

- **Amber:** we have an issue which means that one of our baselines may be missed; however, we are working on it to see if the issue can be resolved. Take this as an early warning though that I may need support to get things back on track.
- **Red:** there is an issue that will cause one of the baselines to be missed. We will be unable to resolve it within the project team and need to escalate for support to get the issue fixed.*

We'll see some examples below of how you apply the RAG statuses in your reporting and what they imply in each case.

REPORTING ON YOUR SCHEDULE

Reporting on your schedule is achieved by taking your baselined milestone plan and reporting progress in relation to that. By way of demonstration, let's use the milestone plan that we baselined earlier in the chapter (Table 7.4, below).

Now that we are in live project reporting mode, the "Date" column becomes your "Baseline date" column. The dates in this column **must not change** (unless, of course, you re-baseline the plan). You then add two more columns that allow us to get a picture of how the project is going. To the right you add a "Forecast/Actual date" column and a "Status" column – and you end up with something like Table 7.5.

The "A" that you see against the first three dates in the Forecast/Actual column denotes that the date is an actual date as the task has completed. You can choose to include this or not, as it is implied by the "Status" of the milestone obviously, but I find it useful to call out.

You can immediately start to infer a story from this milestone report. The foundations completed on time, but the frame completion was delayed by nearly two weeks which has caused a knock-on delay to several subsequent milestones up until the end of the year. The delay is gradually

---

* Incidentally, I should perhaps say that if you *know* you have an issue that will definitely require Sponsor/management support to resolve, do not wait until next month's reporting cycle and use the RAG status to highlight it. You should escalate issues as soon as you realize they cannot be resolved without support from those you are escalating to.

TABLE 7.4

Schedule baseline for a house-building project

ID	Activity	Date
1	Foundations complete	Mar-30
2	Frame complete	May-02
3	Structure is weathertight	Sep-07
4	External construction complete	Oct-18
5	Carpentry/joinery complete	Dec-07
6	Electrics and plumbing signed-off	Jan-31
7	House ready for buyers	Mar-06

TABLE 7.5

Example milestone schedule report

ID	Milestone	Baseline Date	Forecast/Actual Date	Status
1	Foundations complete	Mar-30	Mar-30 A	Complete
2	Frame complete	May-02	May-15 A	Complete
3	Structure is weathertight	Sep-07	Sep-18 A	Complete
4	External construction complete	Oct-18	Oct-31	Amber
5	Carpentry/joinery complete	Dec-07	Dec-14	Amber
6	Electrics and plumbing signed-off	Jan-31	Jan-31	Green
7	House ready for buyers	Mar-06	Mar-06	Green

being clawed back such that the Carpentry is just a week late, and by the time the Electrics and plumbing are signed off, we are again tracking against our original baseline, and the end date is preserved. As milestones 4 and 5 are both within the two-week agreed schedule tolerance they have an Amber status* – if the external construction were delayed by another two days, you would need to discuss re-baselining that milestone with your Sponsor (though hopefully that would be an acceptable change, as the end date remains unaffected).

Hopefully you can see how a few simple metrics very quickly bring the project status to life and will tell a Sponsor a great deal of information in a simple, easily digestible format.

---

* Unfortunately, much of the impact of this will be lost in black and white editions of the book, but for an example of how visually effective this kind of reporting can be, simply look online and search for "RAG status report".

TABLE 7.6

Cost baseline for a house-building project

Activity	Cost
Land purchase	$80,000
Surveys	$2,000
Design	$15,000
Materials	$70,000
Labor	$118,000
Risk	$38,500
Total	**$323,500**

TABLE 7.7

Example cost report

Activity	Baseline Cost	Spend to date	AFC	Status
Land purchase	$80,000	$72,183	$72,183	Complete
Surveys	$2,000	$2,100	$2,100	Complete
Design	$15,000	$18,200	$18,200	Complete
Materials	$70,000	$12,728	$84,700	Red
Labor	$118,000	$7,400	$98,700	Green
Risk	$38,500	$0	$19,250	Green
Total	**$323,500**	**$112,611**	**$295,133**	**Green**

REPORTING ON YOUR COSTS

To report on our costs we follow the same principles as we've just walked through with our schedule. First of all, you start with the baseline you agreed with your Sponsor. Continuing the house-building example discussed earlier in the chapter, we baselined the costs in Table 7.6.

As before, the key for reporting is to report on progress in relation to that baseline. So we add a few columns to the right – Spend to date, Anticipated Final Cost (or AFC), and Status. That gives us the following cost report:[*] Table 7.7.

The Anticipated Final Cost (AFC) is a new concept here, but it is not a difficult one to get your head around. It's simply a forecast of total cost.

---

[*] It is worth distinguishing between a "Cost Report" and a "Cost Plan." Your Cost Plan is your detailed tool for managing every aspect of the costs on your project. The Cost Plan provides information which feeds into the Cost Report – a regular summary provided to the Sponsor of how costs are tracking against baseline.

Just like when looking at your schedule, you have a baseline date and a forecast date, with costs we have a baseline cost, and the Anticipated Final Cost – that is, our forecast for what the ultimate cost of that line item will be, once the project is complete. Your status is based on the difference between the baseline cost and the AFC.

Once again, this simple table in a report tells us everything we need to know about cost and brings the story of the project to life. Everything up to and including the design is complete, so just by looking at this table we can infer that we are in the construction phase of the project. We originally estimated up to $80,000 for the purchase of the land to build our house on. It turns out that wasn't a bad estimate – we bought the land for $72,183, within 10% of our baseline (and fortunately on the cheaper side of the original estimate). That is now complete so the AFC will not change for the rest of the project.

The surveys were slightly more expensive than forecast, but well within a 10% tolerance, whereas the design overspent by over 20%, but is now complete. If it were not complete yet, this would have a red flag and be under consideration for change control (perhaps for the last couple of months, this has been red on the report, but the Sponsor agreed not to take action, given the saving already made on land purchase).

So far, we've only spent $12,728 of our $70,000 budget on materials – a fraction of the money available. But we now have a complete design which can be properly costed, and having done so, we have an estimate from our contractor for material costs. At $84,700 this far exceeds our budget (including tolerance), so it's a red flag. Depending on how the project is being funded, underspend elsewhere might make this acceptable. But let's imagine this is a charity project and a local builders' merchants has offered to provide materials up to the value of $70,000. In this context, the fact that we are forecasting an overspend is a real issue. They have not agreed to provide the $84,700 that we now believe we need to complete the project. The first step is a discussion with the project team and then the Sponsor to work out some options and recommendations.

For now though, let's finish off looking at what this cost report is telling us. Carrying on down, our labor costs are coming in lower than originally anticipated, as we got a final cost from the building contractor based on the completed design, fixed at $98,700. That's well under budget, status is green. We set aside a probabilized risk value of $38,500 to deal with uncertain events. At the moment we haven't had to spend any of it (though one strategy for dealing with our materials cost issue *might* be to use our risk allowance).

But right now, we haven't spent any of it. The project manager takes a view that between now and the end of the project, we might need to use half that allowance to deal with unexpected events, so our AFC is $19,250.

Now we add up the columns. The baseline obviously does not change. Our spend to date gives us a sense of how far we have progressed. At roughly $112k, we have already spent just over a third of our budget. Our total AFC is sitting at about $295k which is great news, as it's well under our original estimate, but we'll need to figure out a plan for the Materials cost before we relax.

Again, I hope this demonstrates how a relatively simple table of information gives you a huge insight into the life of a project.

GENERAL REPORTING PRINCIPLES

Finally, a few general reporting principles for you to bear in mind.

- **Reporting issues is not an admission of failure.** Some project managers I've worked with seem practically allergic to giving anything a red RAG status or escalating issues. They see it as an admission of failure. They feel that to ask for help demonstrates that they are not "managing" the project. Or they feel that presenting a version of the world that isn't all green would not be acceptable. To them I say, "consider the alternative." If you have an issue on your project, you have an issue on your project. There is no getting away from it. By not reporting, you are taking the alternative path and you are now actively *hiding* the issue. So you now have two issues: the original one, and the fact that you will be in a lot deeper water when the original issue comes to light, as you will have known about it and not said anything.

  Worse than that though, you are not making use of one of your primary defenses. The idea of good project management is to have many tools at your disposal to deal with issues when they arise. Reporting is one such tool, and we must not forget the role of the Sponsor and senior stakeholders here. They have charged you with delivering something and as such are invested in its delivery. They are there to **support** you in getting it delivered – not pass judgment when you request help.

Finally, you are not expected to be Superman. You are just expected to deliver the project, and if you need to bring in some extra firepower to do that, then that is still doing the job. It is simply a fact that not all issues will be within your remit, authority, or pay-grade to resolve. Obviously, you should use your escalations wisely – no-one wants to be the project manager that cried wolf. But at the same time, if you asked someone to do something for you, would you rather have the occasional escalation that turned out to be nothing, or find out too late about an issue and then discover the project manager had known all along?

- **Stay true to previous reports.** Reports should provide a sort of narrative for how the project is doing. To that end, once you have established the template for the report, stick to it – don't keep changing your story. Establish what the metrics are and change them as little as possible. This applies across the project, but also from one report to the next. If you said in your report last week that you would do X, Y, and Z, then this week you should report that you did X, Y, and Z. Or that you did X and Y, but were unable to complete Z which will be finished next week. While a report gives a view of the project at a point in time, regular reporting should allow stakeholders to build a sense *over time* of what is going on. That means you must report consistently.
- **Share the report with your team.** It's good practice, and good communications, to share with your team what you are reporting. You might even ask for their input into the report, but you should certainly share with the team what each final report looks like so that they have visibility of how the project (and their work) is being reported to the wider world. It can also form a good talking point for addressing issues and figuring out how to deal with what the report is telling you – as a team.

ORGANIZATIONAL GOVERNANCE

The last aspect of governance that we'll consider is the governance organization. This is the map of people and groups that will be involved in the project and – importantly – what they are *authorized* to do on

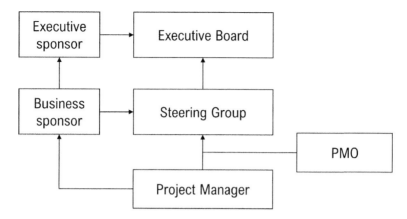

FIGURE 7.2
Typical project organization.

the project. For example, even very small businesses will have different levels of authorization for financial payments. The boss can sign off on any payment, the Finance Director can sign off purchases up to a value of $50,000, while a manager has a spend limit of $5,000 before they need to seek further authority. Often, it will not be a single person, but a group of people – so a Board of Directors might need to meet to make certain decisions, with the decision made by a majority vote.

In project life, this will be the case as well. It is worthwhile therefore to sketch out your project organization at the start of the project and agree up-front who will be responsible for what. See Figure 7.2 for an example of a typical project organization diagram.

STEERING GROUPS AND TERMS OF REFERENCE

On large projects and especially on multi-disciplinary projects that touch several areas of a business or enterprise, it will often be appropriate to convene a Steering Group. For example, if you are undertaking a project which involves organizational change, you might require senior stakeholders from HR, Finance, and Legal to be involved. No one group (or representative) can make decisions that affect all three, so you create a Steering Group with representatives from each. The Steering Group will then be called upon when key decisions are needed on the direction of the project. Also, while the project manager is there to make day-to-day decisions on how resources should be used to deliver the project, it will not normally be within the project manager's remit to make decisions on behalf of the business, or in relation to the wider business as a whole.

When you sketch out the organization you believe you will need to support your project, consider all the questions you might need to answer as you move through the various project cycles and who, within the wider organization, would be authorized to "sign-off" on any given decision. On larger projects it can also be helpful to have a Terms of Reference document, which sounds daunting, but is nothing more than a series of statements about what each part of the project organization is and does, how often they should meet, and how decisions will be made.

EVERYTHING'S FINE UNTIL IT'S NOT

Project governance is both your weapon and your shield. Good project governance will give you the tools and mechanisms to get decisions made quickly, by the right people, based on the right information. In that sense it can be the most powerful weapon in your project management arsenal. It is also the means by which you create the walls necessary to defend your project, and is thus your best form of defense. I cannot overstate its importance – especially on larger projects. Your project will – genuinely – live or die by how well you set up its governance.

Setting up good governance requires a little time and effort, but it is a small price to pay for having safeguards in place that give you early warnings of the dangers ahead. Not everyone understands the value of good project governance. But governance is like a heartbeat in two important ways:

- It helps to set the rhythm of the life of your project and acts as an enabler for all of the vital functions within the project. But more importantly:
- People have a tendency to take it for granted until it stops.

As a colleague of mine remarked recently, "everything's fine until it's not." People have a tendency to be optimistic about projects when things are going well and will fail to see why governance is necessary, especially where it creates an administrative overhead.* Don't be tempted to stop, just because things are going well. Eventually something will happen which will cause you to go back to your governance and when that happens you will be ever so grateful to find the safety net of governance there.

THE EVERYDAY PROJECT MANAGER SHOULD...

- Allow change to happen but only under control.
- Set baselines and defend them.
- Use a regular report to sum up your progress and check you are staying on top of all the different aspects of your project.
- Know your escalation path and don't be afraid to use it.

---

* Which, of course, the very best project governance does not.

Phase 3

Build and Execute

8

Hell Is Other People: Managing the Team

Understanding the key terms and concepts in project management is all well and good, but it will be for nothing if you don't give some consideration to the people who will actually be delivering the work. Projects live or die by the people involved and how they are managed. After all, a project is just a concept and doesn't require management – it is the people that require management. Fortunately, managing a project team well is by far the most rewarding part of undertaking a project, and the reason why the best project managers get up in the morning. This chapter will look at some of the main considerations when managing a team, as well as some of the common pitfalls and things to look out for.

CONSIDERING THE TEAM

In Chapter 4, we considered each of the people on the team from a project point of view. That is, what roles are required on a project team and what *function* each person is required to perform. However, that takes no account of the *personalities* involved in the team and how each personality within the team can best be used to maximize the outcome and success of the project. Therefore, it is worthwhile – actually, no, it's *essential* – to spend some time at the start of the project (and at various points throughout) considering each of the people on the team, how they interact, and how to get the best out of them. Which brings us to the first key point to understand when managing a project.

Ensure the success of others. At all times your main aim should be to help others to be successful. This may require more support for some than others – and often it will require a lot of imagination, patience, and cajoling. Less mature project managers often believe that a project's success is dependent on their own ability to drive things forward through willpower and self-belief. In truth, the most successful project managers spend very little time worrying about how they will succeed and focus their energies instead on how to ensure every member of their team has what they need to carry out their job successfully. And of course it then follows naturally that the team delivers, the project is successful, and the project manager is, in turn, successful. This seems obvious but it is easy to lose sight of, and is worth re-stating. As you consider each member of the team, consider what you can do that will assist them best in doing the thing you need them to do for the project.

Now, some companies invest vast sums of money carrying out aptitude/personality tests of the sort that Myers-Briggs pioneered years ago, and these are often informative and can help a team to understand each other. However, you don't need an expensive consultancy to tell you about your team – just your eyes and ears. Here are a few things to look out for.

The loud ones and the quiet ones. In every group of people there will be those that are more extroverted and those more given to introspection. The loudest voice in the room often draws the most attention, but is not necessarily the most qualified to make their pronouncements. Similarly, just because someone prefers to keep their thoughts to themselves does not mean those thoughts should not be considered by the wider team. Good project managers are adept at balancing the loudest voices and the quietest ones, giving additional amplification to the shy whilst reining in the bombastic nature of the loud. By making project meetings more democratic in nature, you can go some way to achieving that balance. So make sure everyone in the room understands that they have an equal voice. This needs to be borne out by your actions – so if, for example, there is a point under discussion, make sure you have asked everyone in the room for their opinion. This has the dual effect of reducing the volume of the loudest people (if it is clear that everyone will be given the opportunity to speak, they will spend less time shouting their way into the conversation), while increasing the volume of the quietest (who will be given a clear space in which to state their thoughts).

Go back to roles and responsibilities. You'll find that the loudest people will be quite happy to offer their opinion on anything and everything – whether it's their area of expertise or not. By gently referring back to the roles and responsibilities you have a means of stopping one person dominating the discussion, e.g. "That's a great point, Nick. But given this is a design question – Alice, you're our designer: what's your view?"

In the moment, treat all contributions as equally valid. As the project manager, you can decide later which is the path you believe is the most sensible to take. Even if you believe an idea is completely preposterous, it is better to thank someone sincerely for offering it up and later politely discount it, than to dismiss it and have that person lose interest in contributing altogether. Their point here might be preposterous, but the one they make three weeks from now might be dynamite, so you want to make sure people feel their contributions are welcome and valid at all times. Particularly near the start of the project, by treating all contributors equally you will quickly learn for yourself which are the most reliable.

Who does everyone else stop to listen to? More broadly, this is about watching how members of your project team react to one another during meetings and interactions – be aware of the subtle reactions people have and how they talk to one another. But a useful thing to look out for is the one person in the room that everyone listens to. I've worked on a lot of projects where there is one (often quiet and unassuming) person that everyone else will listen to. There's a reason for this: whatever it is they are saying, they're usually right. Whether we do it consciously or not, we are all aware of those people who tend to talk sense, or have their thoughts borne out. So, if there is one person in the room that everyone else seems to be listening to, you'd be well advised to stop and listen to them too.

Who might be out of their depth? Businesses will always – always – try to generate more by doing less. These "efficiencies" are sometimes found by simplifying processes or seeking out cheaper raw materials. But all too often, businesses find efficiencies by trying to get more out of the people that work from them, so instead of hiring a new person, an existing member of staff will simply be given additional duties – whether they are qualified (or even happy) to undertake them or not. Therefore, you may end up with someone on your team who is simply not up to the job. As frustrating as this is, it is often not the fault of the individual and it pays to give them the benefit of the doubt. It is also tempting to dismiss these people as unhelpful or, worse yet, useless or incompetent. However, dismissing someone who (to use football terminology) is being played out of position will not help them, will not help your project, and will not help you. So if you have someone on your team who you think may be out of their depth, think about what could be done to help. Consider some of the following options:

- Buddy them up with someone else who might be able to teach them as they go. This person might be on the project team, or just another person in the organization who is prepared to do a little mentoring.
- Is there some training that could be provided that would help them to deliver on their role? Perhaps it could even be justified as part of the project budget (assuming the cost is not too great).
- Can they be encouraged to do some self-education? Don't forget it is easy to find training videos online for just about anything – often for free.
- Is there an option to switch them? Again, bear in mind this person might not be doing the role by choice and might be deeply unhappy that they are out of their depth. Often, a frank and open conversation with the individual and/or their line manager might help reach an agreement that this is not going to work in the long term and somebody else might be available who would be better-suited. This needn't be a bad reflection on anyone concerned if handled correctly, but rather a group of adults finding a good solution to a project issue that leaves everyone involved happier.

Projects are fantastic opportunities for personal development and for people to get exposure to skills and activities that are outside of their usual role or indeed out of their comfort zone. But this should be done with everyone's eyes wide open, and as a project manager you should ensure you are providing extra support and consideration to those people who might be learning as they go.

WHERE IS THE FRICTION?

It would be fairly naïve to believe that – particularly on large project teams – everyone gets on brilliantly. Most people will put on a professional act, so it can be quite hard to pick up on areas where all is not quite rosy in the garden. If there are two people on your team who cannot abide each other, it will change the dynamic and it will affect their ability to objectively judge each other's contributions. Now, you're not there as a peacekeeper (necessarily), but it is useful to pick up on these interpersonal conflicts. So if you are aware, or become aware over the course of the project, that Connie thinks Joan is incompetent, make sure you temper your judgment with this knowledge. Connie might be slightly quicker to put down Joan's ideas, or slower to do something that makes Joan's deliverables easier to achieve. Given that your primary interest is ensuring the delivery of the project objectives, think about how you can best get Connie and Joan working together in the service of that goal (even if that means allowing them to avoid each other entirely).

It is also worth remembering your own biases in this respect. It would be completely unreasonable to expect that you will get along famously with every single person you encounter – particularly in a work environment where you have to spend time with people you might otherwise choose not to. I have, on several occasions, had to manage people I don't see eye-to-eye with. And I have had to make a conscious effort at times to turn down the voice in my head that is irritated with them, as – regardless of what you think of a person – if you treat them correctly, you will often get what you need from them. If you want to be successful by delivering your project objectives, it pays dividends to be the bigger person. Try not to write off the comments of an individual based on your personal feelings towards them. It can be very frustrating – I have found myself commenting to friends "it's incredibly annoying but so-and-so is absolutely right!" on more occasions than I care to share, but it's one of the necessary evils of good project management.

IS THERE SOMEONE WHO DISLIKES THE GROUP ENVIRONMENT?

Be conscious of how people will behave differently in meetings. Sometimes a one-to-one will be a more effective means of divining information. There is obviously a time/cost/benefit judgment to be made here. Group meetings are useful for getting group input and ensuring certain messages are communicated just once. It is obviously inefficient to abandon a group meeting of eight people in favor of eight individual one-to-ones. Therefore use one-to-ones to dig deeper into an individual's area of responsibility, where doing so in a group environment might be unfair or counterproductive.

It can be especially difficult, too, to raise issues or problems in a group environment – particularly if you feel any degree of responsibility for the issue. For anyone to admit to a mistake in public is much harder than admitting it privately to a manager you trust to behave decently. As that manager, you may find that, for certain questions, you get a completely different answer if you allow someone to save face.

THE PROJECT FIRST-TIMER

If there is a person or people assigned to your project who has not undertaken a project before, be mindful of the fact that certain project structures and terminologies might not be familiar to them. Words like benefits and objectives will assume their everyday meaning, rather than the specific meaning they hold to project managers. If the new team member has previously been used to open-ended work, or an environment where deadlines are not commonplace, they might struggle to understand why you're getting so worked up about a key milestone – or just not have a "delivery" mindset. I have been guilty on several occasions of getting very frustrated with someone before stopping and remembering that they just don't think like a project manager. And why should they? I don't think like a pilot. Or a salesperson. Or a cellist. Everyone has a different skill set and a set of experiences that has conditioned the way they think and react to situations. Including you. If thrown into an orchestra, you might appreciate a friendly cellist explaining to you why it's so important to watch the conductor. It's easy (and reasonable) to get annoyed when people don't understand the world you're familiar with, but the solution lies in explaining why your way of thinking is necessary in the specific environment you're both working in (in this case, the project environment). Because even if this is not their comfort zone, they are in your world now, so they need to understand what are the things to be looking out for, and why they should care.* Think how grateful you would be to that friendly cellist who took the time to explain the peculiarities of performing in an orchestra and then do the same for the people in your team who might need an extra bit of help understanding their place within the team.

MATRIX MANAGEMENT

Often, one of the challenging things about managing projects in complex, modern organizations is that you will need a selection of people on your project team, drawn from several departments or other teams, none of whom report to you as a line manager in their day-to-day life and who frequently have a "day job" that they need to do as well. This set-up, where you are managing people for the project who you do not "manage" on a day-to-day basis, is often referred to as matrix management. See Figure 8.1 as an example, which considers what a project team might look like for an office move.

As you can see from this example, the project manager has several people reporting to her for the purposes of the project, but does not have line management responsibility for any of them. Indeed the project manager herself is accountable to the Sponsor for the purposes of the project, but within the wider organization, she reports to the Head of Projects. So, for example, her annual objectives, personal development, pay negotiations, and so on will be with her line manager (the Head of Projects), but in terms of the day-to-day project progress, she will report to the project Sponsor (the Head of Property).

This sort of set-up is incredibly common on projects where you are assembling a group of people for a defined period of time to deliver an agreed outcome. When the outcome is achieved the project team disbands and the individuals involved go back to their day jobs, or on to the next project with a different combination of people making up the project team.

---

* And it seems almost too astonishingly obvious to state that one way to do this might be to buy them a copy of this book.

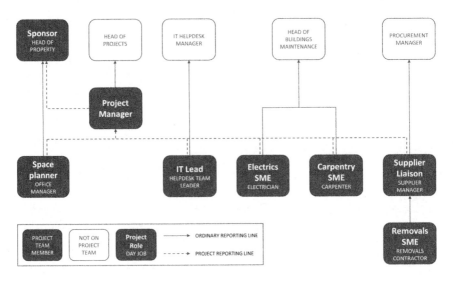

FIGURE 8.1
Matrix management.

If you have a matrix-style project team, here are some additional things you should consider and how they might affect your project:

- Understand that this may not be their day job. You will frequently have people assigned to your project in addition to their day-to-day role. This has two implications.
  - First: they have other things on. Be conscious that there will be people on your project team for whom the project is not their only commitment. They are having to work hard to balance their priorities and you must be supportive of that. More often than not, their day job will need to take priority over project work, so you may find tasks on your project delayed because of work they are doing in their "normal" role. Be patient with these issues – your team member is having to make potentially challenging decisions about which work to prioritize, which will be a source of immense stress for them – and they may not always get it right. But by understanding what their existing commitments are, you have an opportunity to arrange the project work to fit around it, so that neither is put at risk.
  - Second: they may be stepping outside of their comfort zone to be involved in the project. Often people are assigned to a project as an opportunity for development. They are hoping to build on

their existing skills while learning new skills and getting some exposure to a project environment. Understand when members of your team are being pushed (or are pushing themselves) outside of their comfort zone or into an area that they are not wholly experienced in. Again, you should be supportive of this and try to understand why they have taken the project on so that you can help them get the most out of it.

- Build line manager relationships for those in your team. You will need to build a relationship not just with the person working for you but with their line manager. You will necessarily be pulling them away from the day-to-day work in order to assist on your project, so ensure that their line manager is supportive of this. You might need their help freeing up your team member's time to work on the project during a busy period. You should also try to ensure that their involvement in the project is not having a detrimental effect on their other work. Whilst the project may benefit, it should not be at the expense of another area of the business. Work with your team's line managers to make sure everyone gets the best experience from the project and that you have their support – the time will come when you will need it.

- Understand their personal objectives and how your project might fit in. Both of the last two points feed into this final point. Whether they are stepping up to a new challenge, or simply being assigned as the person most suitable for the task, make sure you understand why any matrix team members have been assigned, and how they are being recognized for their efforts. If your team member is being asked to work on your project with no incentive, you will struggle to get the best out of them. Work with their line manager to ensure their work on the project is reflected in their development plan. Maybe they'll receive a small bonus for working on the project. Or fulfill a personal development objective linked to their next pay review. In any case, by working in union with line management, you have an extremely effective tool for ensuring people are appropriately motivated to work on your project.

BEING A (GOOD) MANAGER

We've spent a lot of time looking at the "project" part of being a project manager, but what about the "manager" part? The different ways to manage a project team are as numerous as the people who run them. No two project managers will manage a team in the same way, but all good project managers (and indeed managers in general) would be advised to consider the points covered in the following pages.

YOUR FOCUS: YOU ARE NOT THE EXPERT – FOCUS ON TIME, COST, AND QUALITY

Your job is to manage that project and to that end you have engaged a team of people to carry out certain tasks. Whilst you should take the time to understand what is involved in each of these tasks remember, again, that you are not the expert. Leave it to your team members to do the work of the project. Your job is to manage it – and that means keeping your focus on time, cost, and quality. Your time should be spent reviewing the schedule, the cost plan, and the progress against requirements. As the old saying goes, you don't buy a dog and bark yourself. This can be particularly challenging if you actually have some relevant experience in the field, or perhaps it could still even be your day job. It's not at all unusual for people to work their way up through the ranks from the shop floor to a management role where they are then put in charge of delivering a project. And as part of the project you might have one or more people undertaking work that you know full well how to do, as it used to be your job. It is very tempting – especially when the proverbial hits the fan – to roll your sleeves up and start undertaking tasks on the plan which should be delivered by others. This is – almost without exception – a mistake. Every time you do this you are stealing focus from the management of the project, which should be what concerns you. If you find yourself doing tasks on the project rather than managing it, ask yourself why. Is someone else not pulling their weight? Are you (quite innocently) unable to resist the temptation to get involved? Are you concerned that the quality will not be good enough unless you do it yourself? These are all valid concerns, but the management solution is not to do it yourself. If a builder you employed was running late, you wouldn't get out there and start bricklaying yourself. If the cost of the event you were running became too expensive, you wouldn't get in the kitchen and start doing the catering. I'm not saying that it shouldn't be an option if you're a former bricklayer or caterer. But it should be an option of last resort. First, you should figure out what the issue is that makes you feel you need to get involved in the first place. And if you really must get involved, be aware that you still have a project to run. Do not substitute one activity for the other – you must do both now (hence: it's a bad idea).

FINDING YOUR OWN VOICE

One of the common misconceptions of managing people is that you have to be somehow forceful, domineering, or aggressive in your manner in order to get things done. This is simply not true and it causes some people to "act" at being a manager, putting on a style that is not their own, ultimately alienating others while, unfortunately, believing themselves to be exemplary managers. More and more we hear of people who feel they have "impostor syndrome" – the idea that they are not qualified or do not deserve to be in the role that they are in. I'm sure this gives rise in many cases to people acting according to how they *think* a manager should act, rather than just being a manager. It is vitally important that you do not pretend to be a manager – instead just be you. If you are the project manager on a project then you are the project manager. Therefore, however you behave is how a project manager behaves. You get to define what a project manager looks like – why would you imitate someone else? Now, obviously you want to be a *good* manager and you will need to define what that means to you. But the one piece of advice I cannot emphasize strongly enough is that – however you behave as a manager, make sure you are being you. This means finding your own voice.

There is a story of how the composer Arnold Schoenberg refused to teach George Gershwin. Gershwin's *Rhapsody in Blue* was, at the time, taking the world of jazz music by storm, but Gershwin constantly sought mentors and teachers to help him. Schoenberg's reason for refusing to teach him? Because "I would only make you a bad Schoenberg, and you are such a good Gershwin already!"

I love this story because it is an excellent reminder of the importance of speaking with your own voice. While you should always learn from others and emulate those behaviors in others that you find admirable, you should try to avoid *imitating* them. Find a way to match their behaviors in your own style.

There's also a very good practical reason for doing this. If you are not authentic in your approach to management, you will swiftly lose authority as people can tell very quickly when something is being "put on" for the benefit of those in the room. You need to be you.

Trust me, you are such a good *you* already.

INVOCATION OF AUTHORITY

The subject of authority within a project team is worthy of a whole book in its own right. However, for the benefit of The Everyday Project Manager, I will boil the subject of authority down to two points for your consideration: who has authority (and – briefly – why), and who invokes it.

WHO HAS AUTHORITY?

Authority can be conferred on a person for a number of reasons. Seniority and expertise are the most obvious reasons and the two we'll consider for our purposes here.

Authority through seniority alone will not take you very far.

If you are considered the expert in a given field, what you say is – rightly – given a degree of authority and respect in a way that an amateur *saying the exact same thing* would not. Saying the right thing does not, in itself, grant the speaker authority. That said, saying the right thing *more often than not* will give you a certain amount of authority, as people gradually realize that whatever Fred says usually turns out to be correct.*

Authority, therefore, is usually conferred, as much as anything by behavior. But behaving authoritatively is not just about being decisive, or demanding your own way.

---

* i.e., *who does everyone else stop to listen to?*

WHO INVOKES AUTHORITY?

Invoking authority is when you use someone else's authority as a proxy for your own, e.g. "I'm telling you to do this because Sarah wants it done." It is the worst way in which to attempt to demonstrate authority as it has the exact opposite effect. If you actually have the authority to ask for something, you don't need to invoke anyone else's. People who make a habit of invoking other people's authority will, over time, see their own authority (and to a certain extent, their reputation) eroded.

So why do people use it? Well, there are a couple of good reasons. The first is easier to sympathize with, which is that the person invoking authority genuinely does not feel like they have the right (or authority) to ask what they're asking. They may have been thrown into the position of, say, project manager, because their boss has told them to manage the project, but they don't themselves feel comfortable in the role, or with asking people to do the things necessary to deliver the project. Far easier, then, to say, do it because our boss wants the project done and they just happen to have asked me to be the one to deliver it.

The other reason is a bit more pernicious. Invoked authority is very difficult to argue against, and the people that do so often know that. Imagine if I were to say to you "Can you do X because I spoke to your boss and they made it pretty clear they wanted it done immediately." You are now left in the position of having to trust that that conversation happened and that I have interpreted the demands correctly. There are several things to consider here. Did the conversation genuinely happen? Have I interpreted it correctly – or have I understood the instruction but inflated the urgency? Did your boss specifically ask that *you* do it or did they ask me to do it and I'm just invoking their authority to get you to do it? Did your boss mean that specifically (because maybe it makes no sense)? If you do that and it's not what your boss wanted, could you end up in even more trouble than if you hadn't done it at all?

But it's very difficult for you to argue any of these points without suggesting either that I'm not being completely truthful or running the risk of not carrying out what your boss wanted in the first place. Far better then, if I want you to do something, to ask you on my own authority and, if need be, explain *my* reasons for needing it done. If I do not feel I have a sufficiently good reason to be asking you, then I probably shouldn't be asking you in the first place.

In practice, when someone asks you to do something by invoking the authority of another it is often wisest to get on and do it but, if the opportunity arises, satisfy yourself that this was genuinely the wish of the person whose authority has been invoked. And when you are the person asking others to do things, make sure you understand your reasons for asking them, and then ask them on your own authority, without invoking others.

ACTING ON YOUR OWN AUTHORITY

As a project manager you are in a position of some authority, as you have been selected to lead the project team. You need to manage through all the methods of authority:

- Seniority – show leadership and be confident in your own position. You have the right to ask things of people within the remit of your project.
- Expertise – demonstrate that you have the skills of a project manager by focusing on the things that make a good project manager. Concentrate on managing the delivery of the objectives to the agreed time, cost, and quality – that is what you are there to do. Respect the expertise of others on your team and let them be the experts in their field. Giving others authority in their own areas is a first class way of showing authority in yours.
- Behavior – support your project team to a successful delivery. Lead by example and ensure people know that – provided they are doing their jobs to the best of their ability – you will have their back.
- Don't invoke anyone's authority but your own (if you can possibly avoid it). Very occasionally, it will be necessary to point out that someone very senior wants this job done. But make every effort not to invoke the authority of others when yours will do just fine.

TRICKY TEAM MEMBERS

Every team has its own unique make-up of individuals who behave differently as a group and, when put together, will perform differently from any other group of individuals. Working as part of a team that is performing well is one of the most rewarding things about project management. But of course, there will always be times when certain members of the team make life a little bit harder than it needs to be. As ever, I'll give the benefit of the doubt and say they don't necessarily mean to make life difficult, but whatever their motivation, you would do well to keep your eye on anyone in your team who falls into one of the following categories.

THE SHOW-BOATER

When I was working as an assistant project manager, I was talking with the project manager about one of the team members we worked with, who seemed to enjoy spoiling for a fight in project meetings, while being perfectly reasonable outside.

"If there is a gallery, he will play to it" was the project manager's response. I like that phrase enormously as it so constantly rings true. You will frequently encounter people when you manage projects who will wait until they have an audience before making life difficult. They might wait for a project meeting before dropping a bombshell that could perfectly easily have been raised with you outside the meeting and without the fanfare. It is a self-aggrandizing move. It is designed to show everyone that they are clever somehow, and to demonstrate that they have power. How then, should you deal with a person who won't tell you what's going on until they have an audience?

Perhaps counter-intuitively, the answer is often to give them that audience. They obviously feel the need to demonstrate to you and the assembled company how clever/powerful they are, so let them. Rather than wait for them to drop a bomb under "any other business," give them their own spot on the agenda ("Craig, I recognize how key your delivery is to the project – would you mind giving an update to the team each week?"). It needn't be a public audience either. Perhaps they just don't feel that you are listening to them, so they make their grievances known publicly to force you into a reaction. Maybe set up a weekly one-to-one so they can update you. It helps them to feel listened-to and gives you an early heads-up of any issues that they might otherwise have saved up. Everyone wins.

THE WOULD-BE PROJECT MANAGER

Every so often you will have someone working on your project who wants your job, or thinks they could do it better (or both). They will often use show-boating (see above) to make their point and they almost always think they know best because they have a lot of experience in a specific area to which the project is related. They might have worked on a similar project in the past, or be an expert in a related field. On a couple of occasions in this book I have pointed out that "you are not the expert," and that you should leave the experts to get on with their job while you manage the project. This is the reverse angle. **You are the expert** when it comes to managing the project. If someone else is an expert in their field, then they should content themselves with that, rather than trying to do your job too.

The best way of dealing with such a person is to – gently – remind them of their role within the project team. They have been brought on for a specific purpose and must focus on that. It will do you no harm, ultimately, to emphasize to them how important their piece of the jigsaw is and how much you will appreciate their total focus on the delivery of it.

If need be though, be blunt. You are the project manager and you have been charged with the responsibility for delivering the project. It is not within their remit to review your performance – it is for your managers and Sponsors to make that assessment. They do, however, have a role to play in the project's success. You don't need to run the project to take credit for its success. Remind them of that, and try not to get too frustrated when they do take credit. A project is a team game and everyone gets to win when it's delivered. You win when you do your job as project manager – and everyone else on the team wins when they fulfill their role. As soon as we start trying to do other people's jobs, the whole project fails.

THE OVER-INVOLVED SPONSOR/
CONTROL FREAK STAKEHOLDER

A few years ago, I was asked by my colleague, Sarah, if I would be interested in managing a project she was involved with. She'd assigned someone in her department to sponsor the project, but they didn't have a project manager and she thought this might suit me. She introduced me to the

Sponsor, Karl, who was delighted to have me on board. "This is just what we need! Someone who is willing to take the reins and get this project delivered. No one else has managed to do so yet." I very quickly found out why. I attended one team meeting, after which I took my colleague for a coffee to discuss the Sponsor's behavior in the meeting.

"I'm very happy to manage this project if you would still like me to, Sarah. But you do realize Karl and I can't *both* run it."

You see, Karl was enjoying the role of Sponsor and the perceived seniority that came with it, but he also wanted to dictate precisely *how* the project should be delivered, and had spent much of the team meeting explaining to me (in some detail) how I should go about delivering the project. I had an issue with this, not because my ego was affronted (I'm always happy to take advice), but because the Sponsor is the Sponsor and the project manager is the project manager. You can't be both. If you're the Sponsor, you need to worry about the things a Sponsor needs to worry about, and they are generally many and plentiful.

THE KEYBOARD WARRIOR

Email has become a near-indispensable tool in the early 21st-century office. It's used to communicate, to help establish audit trails, to minute meetings, and much more besides. But it also creates a series of not-so-helpful behaviors. Chief among these, to my mind, is the snot-o-gram. It's genuinely amazing to me how vocal people can be on email whilst refusing to speak out in meetings or when addressed in conversation. I generally don't worry about these keyboard warriors who send lengthy emails (often out of hours, usually copying all manner of people in) detailing their concerns about everything they perceive to be wrong with the project and the way it is being managed.* While the emails are an unhelpful distraction, they normally reflect more poorly on the sender than they do on the person they are writing about.

There are two points to consider here. The first is that just because the manner in which they've written something is irritating doesn't mean it's wrong. Through your annoyance, take a moment to see if they are raising a valid point. I vividly remember a senior project manager one day

* Even if this is not explicit in the email, it's typically implied.

showing me a two-page email criticizing anything and everything about the project, including him. I remember thinking that I would have been furious to receive such an email, but the thing that stuck with me was him calmly saying, "but when you strip away all the bluster and nonsense, these last two sentences are what he's actually trying to say. I should probably have a chat with him about those." Goodness knows, project management is often about being the bigger person, but this was an important lesson. Don't dismiss someone's comments just because their manner is irritating/infuriating. Strip away all the bluster. If nothing is left, you can disregard it.

Which brings us to the second point. Something is bugging this person. Whether or not you choose to agree with what they're writing, your best tactic is to engage them. Why do they feel the need to send emails rather than speak to you directly? One bad apple quickly rots the barrel, so it can sometimes be a good thing that they announce their intentions rather than trying to undermine you without your knowledge. Take the opportunity you've been handed (even if it doesn't seem like one) and talk to them to find out what the problem is. Ultimately, you may still think their "issue" is of no consequence and they are just a troublemaker. It is better to have satisfied yourself that this is the case.

Finally, if you find yourself on the receiving end of a snotty email, do not get drawn into it. If you feel compelled to reply (and often a reply is necessary, to acknowledge to others that you are dealing with it), then keep the reply short and professional. Do not get drawn into a lengthy defense – it is better to acknowledge that your colleague has concerns and offer to meet them to discuss in more detail. If you have witnessed lengthy email debates or games of one-upmanship you will hopefully agree that a short, polite reply is to be preferred – every time. As a manager you will often come in for criticism – it is just part of the job. The trick is to acknowledge that someone has a criticism without accepting or validating it and then move quickly to understand why this person is not happy.

THE ONE WHO ACTIVELY SEEKS YOUR UNTIMELY DEMISE

I'm really sorry to break this to you, but every so often you will encounter a person who, despite your best efforts – and often for no good reason at all – is simply determined that you should fail. And they have appointed themselves cheerleader. Here's the thing: I'm a people person. I can find something in common with most people and have a genuine interest in others. But you can't like everyone. And you can't stand some people. I'm pleased to say that full-on personality clashes tend to be few and far between, but they do happen. Occasionally, you will find yourself working with someone that you are completely unable to build a relationship with. Meanwhile, they will (in some cases) be actively seeking to undermine you, damage your reputation, and see you fail. It's a real shame, but there it is. I wish I had some good advice on this one, but all I can offer is the obvious: try – **try as hard as you can** – to engage them and, to the greatest extent possible, bring them round. But be aware, you cannot win everyone round. Do not invest more than you need to in appeasing someone who will not be appeased. More importantly: do not lose sleep. Do not waste energy. You're doing fine.

And furthermore: you have a project to deliver – if someone is determined to make that hard, so be it. But focus on the task at hand and get the project delivered. If you do that, you prove them wrong and you complete your goal. You win. It's sad they had to make it harder, but sometimes that is just a fact of life.

OTHER BEHAVIORS TO WATCH OUT FOR

It would be lovely to think that everyone spent their entire time acting honorably and in the project's best interests. In real life though, this is not usually the case, and even though – most of the time – people won't be actively working against you, they may not always behave in a manner that is helpful. Of course, the hardest thing about this fact of life is that – by its very nature – this is the sort of behavior people will try and obscure, so it can be very tricky to spot. What follows is a list of watch-outs. These behaviors and actions do not in themselves constitute malice or troublemaking, but after years of working across hundreds of project teams, these are the things I have learnt to look out for as indicators that something *might* be amiss. At an absolute minimum, they should act as a tiny alarm bell, or a reason to dig a bit more deeply into a situation until you can satisfy yourself that all is well.

The passive voice. I am delighted to credit my first mentor in project management, James Mace, with having introduced me to the passive voice. It is an incredibly subtle behavior but once you notice it, you will not be able to stop noticing it. In short, using the passive voice can be a way for the speaker to distance themselves from what is being said. Consider the following two sentences:

- "The report has not been finished yet, so the announcement will need to be made on Friday instead of Wednesday as planned."
- "Mike and I have not finished the report yet, so I think you'll need to make the announcement on Friday instead of Wednesday as planned."

As you may have gathered, these statements ultimately say the same thing, but the first is in the passive voice whilst the second uses the active voice. It's possible that, until you read the second statement, the first seems perfectly reasonable. But when you read the second statement you realize that using the active voice takes ownership of the issue and its resolution. The statement made in the passive voice, however, is intended to obscure both who is at fault for the delay ("the report has not been finished" – **by whom?!**) and who is impacted or needs to take the action to fix it ("the announcement will need to be made" – **by whom?!**) The classic one that I often hear is "the decision was taken to…," or variations on that theme. Often this is used to distance someone from an unpopular decision or one that ultimately proved to be wrong. People who attempt to hide their accountability for actions and decisions should – at best – be treated with caution. Here are some more examples that might seem familiar where the passive voice is being used and your own ears should prick up:

- "It was agreed, long ago, that…."
- "A delay has been caused, which means that…."
- "It is generally agreed that the best approach will be to…."
- "An additional item of scope has been added to the works which needs to be paid for."
- "A higher quality fabric was selected for the seat covers which came at a slightly higher cost."

If you notice someone using the passive voice, there is no need for alarm – there are plenty of people out there for whom this is just another mode of speech. For example, if someone was particularly uncomfortable with confrontation they might not like being so direct as to say "you will need to do this," opting instead to use the passive tense "this needs to be done" and letting you fill in the blanks that it is you who will need to do it. Be wary though of habitual users – it can be a sign they are trying to dodge responsibility. Use of the passive voice is also easily addressed by asking a simple follow-up question – most usually, "Who?" As the passive voice is used to obscure the person behind an activity, you just need to ask for clarity on who that person is/was. For example:

- "Who made the decision to stop the works for one week?"
- "Who needs to speak to the client and tell them about the delay? Is that best coming from me, or someone else?"
- "Who is proposing this approach and why do they think it's our best option?"
- "Who signed off the extra work being undertaken – and were they made aware at the time that it would cost more?"

Taking a few minutes to probe at statements made in the passive tense will often help you to quickly get to the root of an issue. It is a fairly weak attempt to obscure (most people won't even realize they're doing it), so you should also find that you do not have to scratch too hard to get to the underlying issue.

Weasel words. As with the passive voice in general, there are certain specific words that trigger an alarm to go off in my head. Again, they might be completely innocuous, but are always worth a follow-up. If you hear any of the following words, I would advise digging deeper: "think," "probably," "believe," "should," "hopefully," "just." Consider the following:

- "I **think** we **should** have it done for the end of the week," is a very different statement from "We will have it done by the end of the week."
- "I **believe** the reason we're doing this is to increase profits." Well is it, or isn't it?
- "It's **probably** the right thing to do, given the pressure of time we're under."
- "I spoke to the team and they'll **hopefully** have a first draft out by Tuesday."

Put simply, they are all terms that are used to make the statement a little more vague, a little less certain – allowing the speaker some wiggle room if things don't pan out ("I only said we'd *probably* be able to do it!"). If the person building the extension at your home used any of these words whilst updating you on progress, you (as Sponsor) would not be happy. Don't accept them from your project team – and try to avoid them yourself. Project management is all about reducing uncertainty (see also Chapter 9). The way to reduce uncertainty is – wherever possible – to remove vague statements and encourage people to take responsibility and accountability.

You do this, too, by being flexible yourself. If you know that there is some flexibility, consider the following: "Don't tell me it will probably be done on Monday. Especially if you're only saying that because you think it's what I want to hear. How about we say it will definitely be done by Wednesday?" If the contractor genuinely thinks it can *probably* be done by Monday, they will be happy to guarantee its delivery by Wednesday. They are now happier to take responsibility for ensuring its delivery to the new, realistic timescale and you have greater certainty that you will get what you need when you need it (assuming the task was not on your critical path and could be delivered on Wednesday without having an impact on the rest of the project).

The final weasel words are "just" and "only." They are used in the same way, not to increase vagueness, but to undermine (and as a result underestimate) the complexity or effort involved in a task. Consider the following statements:

- "It's **just** an extra three feet to the property boundary; why don't we include that in scope?"
- "I'm **only** asking for two weeks to be taken out of the schedule. Over the course of a year that should be achievable!"
- "It's **just** a matter of getting agreement from the Town Planners and I can't see why they would object."
- "I don't see a problem here. We **only** need to change our approach and we'll be able to get the work done in half the time."

As before, the use of the words "just" or "only" aren't in and of themselves troublesome, but they act as a flag that what follows may not be as simple as someone is trying to make out. Often, the person in question really does perceive the task at hand to be simple – they honestly think it can *just* be done in a day. But they might have no basis for this assumption other than their opinion. Occasionally, a person knows full well that what they're asking is unreasonable, but by using words like just and only they are making it harder for someone to counter. "Why are you being difficult? I'm *only* asking you to sacrifice some contingency...." "Just" and "only" makes it sound like what is being requested is simple and easy to accommodate. Make sure you are happy that's true.

False urgency. Be wary of anyone who tells you for the first time today that a task had to be done three weeks ago or who regularly prefixes their messages with the word **URGENT**. If you are being asked to drop other activities and prioritize a supposedly urgent task, it is not at all unreasonable to ask what the reason for the urgency is. Be especially skeptical if the reason given is "because so-and-so said so." Refer back to Invocation of Authority earlier in this chapter for more on this but, when you think about it, "because someone said so" is not actually, of itself, a cause for urgency. Why has this person requested it be prioritized and are they aware of the impact of prioritizing this work? Because most things in project life come down to a trade-off.

The way to counter false urgency (and to a certain extent real urgency) is first to question the reason for the urgency. If nothing else, this will give you a better understanding of why you're being asked to prioritize a task over your other work, and it may lead to you offering up an alternative way to reduce the urgency without having to re-plan the whole project.

The second thing to do is to point out that (as will almost certainly be the case) in order to get a new thing done urgently, something else will have to suffer. Ask, "just to confirm, are you happy for me to get Task A done on the basis that I will now have to get Task B done next week, rather than this week as originally planned? And that means that Task C might not be completed in time either." Again, if nothing else, it means that when Tasks B and C are delayed you can be clear that you advised this was a likely outcome of prioritizing Task A. It is not catastrophizing to say that other things will suffer if you have to change priorities. It is the responsible and sensible thing to do, to point out the impact of changes and ensure everyone's expectations are set accordingly.

Deflection. When things get tricky, we all have a tendency to put defensive measures into play. As a project manager you will be faced with instances where you need to get to the bottom of an issue which will mean squirreling your way around peoples' natural defenses. When difficult questions are being asked, deflection is a quick and dirty, go-to option for a lot of people and something that you will need to be on the lookout for.* Put simply, deflection is not answering the question. But it's possible for people to not answer the question while appearing as though they have. Be alert for:

- Subject changes:

"Has the exhibition caterer come back to you yet confirming they can manage our order?"

"Well, I'm pleased you asked. Everyone's so excited about it. As it happens, we've just taken delivery of the first batch of exhibition flyers. Have you seen them? Here, take a look...."

- Answering questions with questions:

"Has the exhibition caterer come back to you yet confirming they can manage our order?"

"Has anyone from Finance sent them a Purchase Order yet?"†

- Answering a different question to the one that was asked:

"Has the exhibition caterer come back to you yet confirming they can manage our order?

"I spoke to them just earlier. They are absolutely thrilled to be on board and have suggested a tasting session a couple of days beforehand. I told them that sounds great."

In short, when you ask a tricky question, listen to the answer, but at the back of your mind just check that the answer you are being given does in fact answer the question asked. Not listed above, because it deserves a paragraph of its own, is the worst kind of deflection...:

Assignment of blame. This form of deflection is always, without exception, unhelpful. When things have gone wrong on a project, it is entirely appropriate – indeed often necessary – to understand what went

---

* By the way, full marks if you picked up on the passive voice at the start of the sentence. I meant, of course, "When *you* are asking difficult questions...."

† This is a short-term strategy, just enough to wrongfoot you. Therefore, it is usually quickly followed by, or combined with, a subject change.

wrong, and in some cases, who should hold the liability for that failure. There may be damages involved, for example, and it then becomes an unpleasant necessity to understand which organization or individual was at fault. But understanding the root cause of an issue after the event is a different thing entirely from casting blame during. While an issue is ongoing, the important thing is to identify what has gone wrong and what the available options are to resolve it. If anyone on the team appears more interested in deciding who to blame, I would put their thoughts to one side. Agreeing who is at fault does not help you resolve the issue in any way. As I say, occasionally it is necessary to identify who or what was culpable for an issue but it is unhelpful in the extreme to do this whilst the issue is ongoing. What is more, once the issue is resolved you'll find people approach the question of blame with calmer heads and a little more perspective which is incredibly important when dealing with something that might have financial or career impacts for those involved.

Other people's behavior is not a defense of one's own. "I saw that Jim has done it like this so that's how I have done it too," seems like a plausible defense of someone's behavior without closer inspection, but it is not. It is an attempt to absolve the speaker of responsibility for their actions by indicating that a precedent has been set. And so it might have been, but that is not proof that it's the right thing to do. A variant of this is "we've always done it this way and nobody's complained before." This is particularly relevant when you come in fresh to a project and may find out that you have to point out some things that are not working so well. For example, I worked on a project where somebody's job was to go around getting updates each week and keep the plan up-to-date. They appeared to spend a great deal of time doing this, but very rarely actually shared or circulated an updated plan.* When I finally got hold of a copy of the plan I pointed out that several of the tasks were shown in the past (giving the impression they had been completed) when they quite clearly had not been done. The defense given was that he'd always kept the original dates as "everyone knew" the tasks weren't completed, but it didn't seem sensible to re-forecast until we had a better idea of when they would be done. This is patently absurd, but a genuine, real-life example. The defense of "everyone knew" and "I've *always* kept the original dates" justified themselves in this

---

* This was my first warning sign.

chap's mind. If he had said that "the last person to do the job did it like this," he would have completed the set. This was not a daft person. He knew how the job should have been done, and perhaps realized that he should have been flagging the fact that the tasks were not complete. However, he did not feel accountable for the tasks slipping, and had genuinely been doing it this way for a while without anyone complaining, so he kept on going. Before he knew it, he'd lost sight of what he should have been doing and was just having informal catch-ups with people but – crucially – not updating the plan.

IT'S ALL ABOUT THE PEOPLE

Managing people is the most challenging and the most rewarding part of project management. It is – by some distance – the best part of the job, and the relationships you build over the life of your projects will sometimes last a lifetime. At the very least they will teach you a lot about human nature and – most importantly – about yourself. Remember to consider, analyze, and adapt to the behavior of others. Above all though, think carefully about your own behavior, as it will have a direct effect on the outcome and success (or otherwise) of the project. As project manager your behavior sets the tone for the whole project. That is a wonderful gift, a tremendous opportunity, and a well-intended warning.

THE EVERYDAY PROJECT MANAGER SHOULD...

- Listen to what your team is telling you and watch how they interact with each other (and with you) in order to get the best from them.
- Use your own voice.
- Create and act according to your own authority. Do not invoke the authority of others.
- Be on the lookout for misleading, or downright deceitful, behaviors.
- Ensure the success of your project by supporting your team and ensuring each individual is successful in their role.

Phase 4

Project Closure and Lessons Learned

9

Managing Uncertainty: A Brief Introduction to Risk Management

WHAT ON EARTH COULD GO WRONG?

At this point you have just about everything that The Everyday Project Manager needs in their toolbox to manage a project. The only thing we haven't considered is: what if something goes wrong? It is all very well having a plan that works fine on the basis that everything goes swimmingly and all things fall into place. But anyone who has existed on earth for more than ten minutes will know that things don't always go your way. It stands to reason therefore that the world of project management would need to come up with a means of managing and dealing with the little uncertainties that life can throw at you. This is the world of risk management and is, at its most simple, a process for figuring out what could possibly go wrong, working out a response, and then prioritizing your efforts so that **most*** of the things that might imperil your project are being dealt with before they have a chance to hurt you.

In the real world, risk management is a complete discipline in its own right and some projects employ full-time risk managers who have a deep understanding of how to manage risk. Given that there are whole books written on the subject, what follows is a necessarily "light" overview, but I

---

* It's a nice idea but, unfortunately, you will never be able to manage **all** of the risks that might threaten your project. And it's Murphy's Law that – from time to time – the thing that becomes an issue is the one thing that you never considered.

hope to impart some of the principles of risk management that will allow you to reduce and manage some of the uncertainty in your own projects. It is simple common sense that, if achieving the project objectives is important, some time should be spent considering the various things that might stop you doing so. And that's risk management.

DEFINING A RISK

There is a school of thought that project management *is* risk management. You identify your objectives and then set about removing anything which might stop you achieving them. Which is precisely what risk management is. A risk is generally defined similarly to this:

> "A risk is an uncertain event which, if it were to occur, would have an impact on the objectives of the project."

It's worth breaking that sentence down. Let's start with "a risk is an uncertain event." So a risk is simply a thing that might happen whose nature we don't fully understand. "Which, if it were to occur" – so a risk is a thing that hasn't happened – yet. This is important, because you will find people often fail to make the distinction between risks and *issues*. If it hasn't happened yet, it's a risk. If it's already happened or is happening now, it's an issue. The distinction is important because how you analyze and deal with a risk is typically different to how you would deal with an issue. More on that later. The final bit though is perhaps the most important: "would have an impact on the objectives of the project."* Now, you can guess the key part of that sentence that a lot of (often experienced) people overlook. **The objectives of the project**. This is one of those elements of project management which seems self-evident once you know it, but frequently gets lost in the noise and the drama of project delivery. I have been in countless risk management workshops where all manner of

---

* Formal risk management considers all impacts – be they positive or negative. Positive impacts are the opportunities that might be pursued during the life of the project. For example, if such-and-such were to happen we could create significant additional benefit for a small investment of additional effort. However, for the purposes of *The Everyday Project Manager*, I will focus on negative impacts i.e., things that might go wrong.

catastrophic scenarios are discussed at length, only for someone to point out that, actually, if any of these things happened, we could still deliver the objectives of the project.

THE RISK MANAGEMENT PROCESS

The process for risk management is usually described as a cycle, with four components:

- Identify (or capture).
- Analyze.
- Mitigate/implement response.
- Review and monitor (Figure 9.1).

Let's take a closer look at each of these stages.

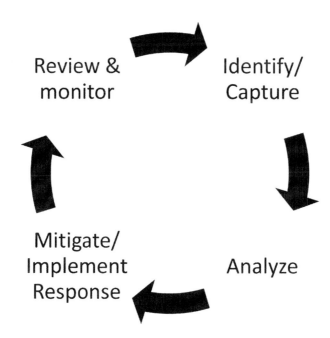

FIGURE 9.1
The risk management cycle.

IDENTIFYING RISK

This is the most straightforward element: simply get a group of people together and consider all the things that might go wrong. This is usually a workshop-style activity that involves getting all the project team in a room, though it could equally be achieved with just the project manager, sitting on their own, coming up with risks. The point is to start figuring out all the things that could stop you achieving your objectives. There is no need to overcomplicate here; simply make a list of the things that could go wrong. For a small project, identifying around ten risks should be more than enough to be going on with. In most cases you'll find a top three very easy to come up with, but if you've got five and are racking your brain for others, don't worry. Carry on through the process with the ones you've got – you're bound to think of more when you next go through the cycle.

ANALYZING THE RISK

The next step is to analyze each risk in turn. The analysis exercise is straightforward – it is done by scoring the risks. Taking each risk in turn, you give them a score for the impact and the probability. My preferred approach is to score the risks between 1 and 4 for impact and for probability. Project and risk managers use a Probability/Impact Grid (or PIG, rather pleasingly) to get a score for each risk. You can set your own criteria for what constitutes a 1 versus what constitutes a 4, but you might like to use the Probability/Impact Grid in Figure 9.2 to get you started.

IMPACT		1: Unlikely 0% - 20%	2: Fairly unlikely 20% - 50%	3: Fairly likely 50% - 80%	4: Highly likely 80% - 100%
	4: At least one objective would not be achieved	9	10	14	15
	3: A change would be required to maintain delivery of the objectives	6	8	11	12
	2: Time, cost and quality baselines could be maintained, but not without significant re-planning	3	5	7	8
	1: A small impact to time, cost or quality but the baseline could be easily maintained	1	2	4	6
		PROBABILITY			

FIGURE 9.2
The probability/impact grid.

The reason for using scores from 1 to 4 is that when people are struggling to assess a risk there is a natural tendency to go for the middle score. By not *having* a middle score you remove that option which means you won't have a whole bunch of risks sitting in mid-table when you complete your assessment (or at least if you do, it's less likely to be a result of lazy scoring).

Each risk has a score assigned to it based on the impact and the probability of that risk occurring. The impact is in relation to the objectives (i.e., it will cost $5,000 more to achieve the objectives; or it will take another month to achieve the objectives; or the objectives can be achieved on time and within budget, but the quality will suffer). You then refer to the grid to get an overall score for the combined probability and impact (so in our example, a risk with an impact score of 3 and a probability score of 4 will have an overall score of 12).*

You may have noticed that the Probability/Impact Grid does not treat probability and impact equally. A greater weighting is given to the impact that a risk has. Some find this counter-intuitive arguing that the more likely a risk is to occur the more prominence it should be given, and that would seem to make sense. If you're pretty sure something is going to happen, you should be doing something about it, right? However, consider the following two risks:

- A risk that is highly unlikely to happen but, if it did, would derail your entire project.
- A risk that will almost certainly happen, but whose impact can largely be absorbed.

When you consider these two extremes it hopefully makes it obvious that you would want to spend your time and energy mitigating the first risk, even though it is unlikely to occur.

You will now have a list of risks that has been scored. Before you even begin to mitigate, just by going through this process so far, you will have a much better handle on the things that threaten your project than you did at the outset. As I've said elsewhere, project management is about reducing surprises, so you are already in a better position than most simply by having considered these things.

---

* It is also an example of a situation where 2 + 2 really does equal 5.

That said, it's one thing to be aware of the things that might scupper you. The next step is to work out what to do about them.

MITIGATING THE RISK

The next stage in the process is to identify mitigation strategies for each of your risks. In an ideal world you would figure out and implement mitigation strategies for every risk on your list, but there is a trade-off to be had here. Effort spent mitigating risk is effort that could be spent working on delivering the actual tasks on the project. Thus you will need to make a judgment as to how much effort (and time and cost) should be expended on mitigating risk. You should definitely spend **some** time on it though and for The Everyday Project Manager, taking your top three risks and working on mitigating them is probably sufficient.

What, then, does mitigation look like? Mitigating risks means undertaking activities that alter the impact or the probability of a particular risk occurring. There are four main mitigation responses to a risk: avoid, reduce, transfer, and accept.

- **Avoid:** is there something that can be done that will allow you to avoid the risk altogether? For example, you have a project restoring a vintage car. You want the project complete by Spring so that you can use it to drive your daughter (who is getting married) to her wedding. Because of the nature of the work, your original plan was to work outside, but there is a risk that you will frequently have to stop work due to bad weather during the winter months. There is now a risk that the stoppages due to weather will mean the project is not completed in time for the Spring deadline. But by hiring some space at a workshop, you can bring the work indoors and avoid the risk altogether. By avoiding the risk created by the weather, you protect the delivery of your objectives, but it is not without cost. The hire of the workshop may not come cheap. You will need to make a decision as to whether the cost of the workshop hire is worth the risk avoidance or whether you will save the money and hope for an unseasonably warm and sunny winter. For more on this, see Budgeting for Risk below, but for now, understand that risk management is not always (or even usually) free.

- **Reduce:** it might be that you cannot eliminate the risk altogether but, by taking certain steps, you may be able to reduce the impact that the risk has, or the probability that it will occur. In practice, out in the real world, most risk mitigation falls into this camp. When you analyzed the risk you already gave some thought to its impact, so now you build on that to think about ways in which that impact could be reduced. Using the car restoration example above, let's say you cannot justify the expense of the workshop, so the weather risk cannot be avoided. However, by erecting a tarpaulin over part of the back yard you are able to weatherproof the area to a small extent. You have not avoided the risk, but you have reduced its impact and certain tasks will be able to go ahead regardless of the weather, whereas you would have had to stop work on them before. It will take you a day to put the tarpaulin up, which is a day you're not working on the car, but you think this is a reasonable trade-off for the time you'll save in the long run.

- **Transfer:** another way to mitigate *your* risk is to transfer it. This is where you create a situation where the impact of the risk is transferred to somebody else (either partially or completely). This is not as good a strategy as avoidance or reduction as you are actually doing nothing to stop the risk in its tracks, or to slow it down. The risk could have the same probability of occurring and the same impact – it's just it will be felt by someone else.

  Back to the car restoration example, one of the parts you need is due to be received on the 12th by your parts supplier, who will then ship it on to you. You need the part by the 20th, and recognize a risk that the part could be received late by the supplier. If they receive it any later than the 18th, they will not be able to get it to you in time using normal shipping methods. So you come to an agreement. The supplier commits to a delivery date of the 12th, but if that date slips beyond the 14th, they agree to courier the part to you same day. You have now transferred (some of) the risk of late delivery to your supplier, as they will take the hit to ensure your schedule is unaffected.

- **Accept:** the final strategy is not really a mitigation strategy at all, but needs to be considered nonetheless. Sometimes there is nothing you can do about a risk other than recognize its existence and the fact that if it were to occur there is very little you can do about it. Or it might be that there is plenty you can do, but you are not prepared to invest the additional cost required to mitigate. In this case, you might agree that spending another $400 will mitigate the risk, but you're not prepared to spend that, so you must accept the risk and agree to deal with the consequences if it happens rather than mitigate up-front. This is obviously not a popular strategy, or a recommended one. However, on some projects, at some points, acceptance might be your only option.

I have laid these strategies out broadly in the order that you would wish to deploy them – if you can't avoid the risk, reduce it. If you can't reduce it, transfer it. And if you can't transfer it, you may have to, reluctantly, accept it.

Your job now is to work through your risks in order of priority, and work out what you can do to mitigate each risk – can it be avoided? If not, is it possible to reduce the impact?

Finally, each of your mitigation strategies will need to be weighed up to see if the effort involved in mitigating the risk is considered worthwhile.

REVIEWING AND MONITORING THE RISKS

The final step in the risk management cycle is to review and monitor risks. The world is constantly changing, and the thing that kept you awake at night last week is of almost no consequence this week. Life changes all the time and so do projects, so it is important to review your risks from time to time. As part of the review you should:

- Consider the scoring for each risk. Is it still right, or have events moved on so that the impact or probability score has changed?
- Have your top three risks changed? Do you need to be diverting efforts to a new risk?
- Has your mitigation been effective? Is there something more you need to be doing? Or should you change tack altogether?

And when you have reviewed your existing risks, you are back to the start of the process – identifying risks. What's new? What could threaten your delivery today that was not an issue last time you considered your risks?

BUDGETING FOR RISK

Management of risk, though, is not without cost. Even just thinking about and understanding the risks on your project takes time out of your day and therefore has a cost. But what is also clear is that it is prudent to set some cash aside to allow you to undertake activities that do not deliver the project, but *de-risk* it. If you just budget for the tasks that need to be done, then you are making the implicit assumption that everything will go well. To use the earlier example, if you were to focus purely on restoring the car then there is no way you would include "purchasing a tarpaulin" in your cost plan. But by allowing a certain amount of risk to be included in your budget, you can pay for things that help you keep your project on track, or even deliver sooner. It is extremely prudent therefore to include a budget line for risk in your project costs – but how should it be calculated?

There is no right answer to that question, but I will suggest two tried-and-tested methods.

One way is to use your risk scores, calculated earlier, to assess the amount of money to be set aside. This method uses the laws of probability to calculate a risk figure that will allow you to mitigate most risks. It is not bulletproof and you may still have a risk materialize that blows your risk pot. But it does allow you to set money aside to cover the most likely eventualities without tying up large sums of cash for things that are uncertain ever to happen.

The method is very simple. For each risk you have identified (or, if you are pressed for time, your top five or top ten risks) estimate how much it would cost if that risk materialized. You have already made an assessment of the probability and all you do now is multiply the two. If you have a risk that would cost you $25,000 if it materialized, but has just a 20% chance of occurring then you should set aside $25,000 × 20% = $5,000. Do this for each of your risks and then add up the amounts set aside. That is your risk budget.

The total amount will be insufficient if all of the risks came to pass, but it ought to give you enough to deal with most risks if they were to appear. And it has been calculated according to the probability of any given risk appearing, so it does not tie your money up, but assumes a likelihood it will be needed.

The other approach is to calculate the cost to *mitigate* each of your risks. The cost to mitigate a risk should be smaller than the cost of the risk materializing (or it's not really an effective mitigation). Again, add up the total cost to mitigate. You can now either factor in probability, pick your top three, or set the entire amount aside and start mitigating (probably depending on the constraints of budget). If you do go down this road though, it is well worth assigning the money to actual tasks and actively mitigating the risks – rather than just leaving the money in the pot until the risk appears.

So far then, you have two options for a risk budget. Both are valid and they each give you a sensible amount of money to use on managing your risks that has a little (if not a lot of) science behind it.

There is a third option (not advised, but often used) which is to pick a number out of the air that you think ought to cover you. One (again, often used) way of doing this is to take a percentage of your total project cost (say, 20%) and add that as a risk budget. While this is not the best way of working out a risk budget (this is a massive understatement), it is definitely better than having no risk budget at all and may actually do just fine for most projects. It is not easy to defend this sort of risk budget if someone chooses to examine it, but it is by no means invalid and certainly better than nothing.

RISKS THAT ARE NOT RISKS

I think it is useful to highlight two examples of risks that crop up all the time, but are in fact not risks.

Risks versus concerns. It seems obvious to say but, during risk identification, make sure you are actually talking about risks. People have a tendency to raise all sorts of things as risks that might better be characterized as concerns. A risk has an impact on the project objectives. There are plenty of things that will concern people, and that they will raise in a risk meeting, that have nothing to do with the objectives of your project. Make sure you keep the conversation focused on project risks – you're not here to fix all the ills of the world. That being said, this does not mean that the concerns are invalid. Give them the attention they deserve. It is far better to allow someone five minutes airtime to talk about a genuine concern of theirs, than to shut it down and lose their input altogether. As ever, be delicate in your handling and you will be fine: make the person feel they are being listened to, while at the same time reminding everyone of the objectives – and if the risk does not affect these you can, perfectly politely and in a manner that does not stifle future contributions, redirect the concern.

Project versus operational risks. Similar to the above, make sure that a risk that has been raised is actually a risk to your project and not a wider business or operational risk. There is sometimes very little daylight between these two ideas, but it is well worth understanding what is a risk to your project delivery and what is a risk to the day-to-day area in which your project happens to be delivered. An example, again using the car restoration project. You might consider that there is a risk that so much of your time is diverted to the car, that you start to miss your weekly movie night with your partner. This is certainly a shame – and you should endeavor to avoid it. But actually, if you miss your weekly movie night, the project objectives are not endangered (in fact, arguably, they benefit from you missing movie night). There is nothing to suggest that, by missing movie night, the project objectives cannot be delivered. However, there is a real and present danger to your *everyday* life. This is not unimportant – of course it isn't – but, from a purist's perspective – it is not a project issue to resolve. Ensure that when you are looking at project risks that they actually are project risks. By all means, go after the day-to-day risks too – these will be important to you and for very good reasons. But recognize also that they are not for the project to resolve.

THE EVERYDAY PROJECT MANAGER SHOULD…

- Spend time considering all the things that might endanger the delivery of your objectives.
- Score your risks according to impact and probability, then focus on mitigating each.

- Be mindful of things that look and sound like risks but are not for your project to fix.
- Budget for risks so that you do not have to find additional funds when a reasonably foreseeable event occurs.
- Implement your mitigations – but don't waste time trying to mitigate every last risk.

10

In Extremis: How to Manage Difficult Projects

NOT ALL PROJECTS ARE CREATED EQUAL

In an ideal world, we'd all be managing projects that were perfectly set up for success and proceeded smoothly without any unexpected interruptions or surprises. Needless to say, this is not the case, but it is worth recognizing that your project will always fall somewhere on a spectrum. The perfect project does not exist and even the very worst projects have a redeeming feature and will deliver something (even if it does not remotely resemble the original intent). Unfortunately for a lot of project managers, you also don't always have the benefit of setting the project up yourself. You inherit a whole mess of assumptions, errors, and disasters that you must now resolve.

The next chapter focuses on what you can do when you take on a project that might not have had the best start in life.

FIRST AND LAST

Whenever a project runs into issues, the best thing you can do is go back to basics and review the objectives. As the project manager, *that* is what you are there to deliver, and in the excitement and stress of a project going wrong it can be quite easy to lose sight of what you had originally set out to do.

Of course, you shouldn't assume that someone has already done the work of outlining the benefits and objectives for the project, let alone the wider vision in which they sit. I have witnessed (and in some cases taken over) projects that had been running for some considerable time without any clearly defined mission statement.

It would also be a mistake to think that because a project has been running for so long without these things being defined that it is too late to sit down and define them now – even if it means "retro-fitting" your objectives and benefits to what has already been delivered to date.

Go back to the objectives and ask: what is stopping us from achieving these and, given the circumstances, how do we make changes so that we can still deliver them. When it comes to the changes that must be made, don't be afraid to think creatively and come up with completely new ways of achieving the original objectives. Hopefully, all that is required is a small course correction to get you back on track, but you should consider every possible option – provided it gives you a route back to your objectives.

If a solution to the specific issue is not immediately obvious, consider what can be done in terms of the Holy Trinity – time, cost, and quality. What is the trade-off that might be required to get you back on track?

- "We can definitely fix this issue and deliver what was asked for, but it will require a little more time and money."
- "If it is essential that this is delivered on time, would it still meet the objectives if we switched to a different material (like quick-setting concrete, for example)?"

I honestly believe that there are very few project issues that cannot be resolved, or at the very least made clearer, by referring back to the objectives and benefits (i.e., what are we trying to do and why are we trying to do it?) and, following that, by considering the Holy Trinity of time, cost, and quality to establish which levers are available to you.

PROJECTS THAT ARE ALREADY FAILING WHEN YOU TAKE OVER

When a project is failing, the decision is often taken to replace the project manager and bring someone else in to rescue the job. If you have managed a few projects successfully – or you just happen to be in the wrong place at the wrong time, this may mean that you are drafted in to a project which is already widely considered to be failing, or even to have already failed. Fear not – believe it or not, these have been amongst my favorite projects to manage. They allow you to really stretch your project management muscles and bring all of the elements to bear that we have discussed in previous chapters.

Of absolute paramount importance in these situations are communication and engagement. When you walk through the door, establish who is on your team and talk to each of them individually to find out their take on the project – starting with the project Sponsor.* Several of them will use the opportunity to moan at what a disaster the project has been and how all attempts to rescue it are pointless. Some will offer genuine insight into the failings and the causes of failure, but may not be well placed to offer up solutions. Others will be positive about the project's prospects, whether that positivity is well-founded or not. But by speaking to everyone individually and picking up on the common themes, you will quickly get a sense of where the issues lie. Listen to what they are telling you. Don't be tempted to offer solutions – yet. You'll get to them later, as a team.

It is highly likely that a team on a failing project will be feeling embattled and morale will be low, so in each of your conversations, be absolutely clear that you understand what a challenging time it must have been, but that you are now taking full ownership of the project and you are confident that many of the issues can be addressed (because this will certainly be the case). It is such a simple statement to make, but it will pay dividends in terms of team morale. Even before you've done anything, you will be setting the project on a new footing.

WHICH SHIPS HAVE ALREADY SAILED?

The next task is to establish what definitely **cannot** now be done. It is highly likely that if the project has been drifting or has been poorly managed for

---

* One of the first things to discuss with the Sponsor are the benefits and objectives of the project. If they struggle to articulate what they are, you have identified your first issue and a good place to start in getting the project back on track.

a while, that an imminent milestone or deliverable is being worked on furiously despite the fact there is no prospect of delivering it. It's time to have a "grown-up" conversation (as one of my old managers liked to call them) and deliver the bad news. Except this isn't bad news. Being honest about what the project can and cannot now deliver is the first step to getting it back on track and safeguarding the delivery of the remainder. It may also be that it's not that it can't be delivered ever – just not to the stated deadline. Obviously, you will have discussed it with your team and considered all options and levers for maintaining the deadline, but it is time to communicate that the deadline cannot be met. Two things count in your favor here. First, an incoming project manager on a failing project usually has a honeymoon period in which to bring out a few dead bodies without their own abilities being questioned. Second, this is, quite simply, good management. Given the inherited facts of the matter, stating that a deadline can't be met (and either agreeing to abandon it or simply missing it as you predicted you would) *cannot* be bad management. Pretending that a deadline can be met, when you know full well it can't, is very much bad management.

WHAT AREN'T WE TALKING ABOUT?

Once you have a feel for the project that you have taken over, it is important to be conscious of what people are not saying, as well as the things that they are. People are very quick to talk about the big, obvious issues (in their mind), and rightly so. Often though, these are the tip of the iceberg. Believe it or not, the first thing that people start shouting about is usually a distraction. It is usually a proxy for the real issue though. If the big issue has a relatively straightforward solution, you should actually worry a bit more.* If the solution was so straightforward, why hasn't it been fixed already? The answer is: because it isn't the *real* issue.

After a couple of days getting up to speed, people will have given you a broad overview of the project. They will have spoken about all the elements of the project and probably had a shout about the same big issues facing

---

* Sorry to burst your bubble. It's deflating when you think you can easily turn the project around only to realize the real issue has been lurking in the shadows.

the project. Are there any elements that seem important to you, but which people aren't talking about? If it is important, people should be telling you about it. In a lot of cases, this will be because that element is actually fine, but in some cases, people aren't talking about it precisely because the solution isn't straightforward and they don't know how to articulate that. Or it might just be that people have a gut feeling something is wrong, but don't want to raise it without some evidence. If people have an instinctive feeling that something is not right, that is often worth investigating. Go with *your* instincts – what is the item which would appear to be important, but doesn't seem to get much airtime. Dig deeper to make sure that the reason people are quiet on the subject is genuinely because there's nothing to see here, and not because they don't know how to tell you.

GETTING THE MESSAGE OUT

The important thing is not to sit on messages that are uncomfortable or might be deemed bad news. The chances are that, if you have been asked to take over, people will be expecting you to pop up at some point and explain that things aren't all that rosy in the garden. However, it is also important to deliver that news appropriately. First of all, before you deliver a difficult message, make absolutely sure that the message you are delivering is true. If one person has told you that the plan is shot to pieces and the objective cannot possibly be achieved now, no matter how convincingly that message is delivered to you, do **not** immediately parrot it to others. First, satisfy yourself that this is definitely the case. Talk to others in the team to confirm they share that view. Look at anything that might provide evidence to support that claim. When – and only when – you are clear that there is an issue here, there is a further step you must take.

It is not sufficient to tell people that there is an issue. That is the first part of a three-part message that you will need to communicate. It is an important part though – by establishing the issue and being able to articulate it clearly and demonstrate *why* it is an issue, you bring people on board for the first part of the journey. The second part is the resolution. Work with your team and figure out the options for resolving the issue. There's more than one way to skin a cat, and it is worth coming up with a couple of options that could be undertaken to resolve the problem. Be open to left-field ideas; you're trying to fix a tricky project and what starts as an oddball idea might give way to an inspired one.

Try to get two or three options on the table. If you have more than three, that's fantastic, but now it's time to whittle them down to your top three. If you only have one option, that's not so great, but at least your way forward is undeniable. The final part is to figure out the impact of implementing your rescue plan. Something will have to give – either you're going to need a bit more money, or the schedule needs to slide, or part of your scope needs to go. For each option, work out what is needed to achieve it. What needs to be sacrificed to get this project back on the right track?

Now you are ready to take the options to your Sponsor (or Steering Group) to present your three points:

- I have identified this issue.
- Here are the options for what can be done to resolve it (along with the team's recommendation).
- Please advise how you would like us to proceed.*

That is how you deliver the message, and note that the final point is to put the ball back into the court of the Sponsor. As the person with overall accountability for the project, it is the Sponsor who must decide on the course of action – and take responsibility for that decision.

You might need to do this a few times as things get unearthed (or preferably once, but for a few issues). In any case, you now have a plan to move forward. Here are a couple of other things to consider as you pick up the reins.

WHAT'S THE MORALE LIKE?

If you've ever worked on a demoralized team (or even just felt demoralized), you should be aware of how important good morale is to getting a job done, and how corrosive poor morale can be. If you are joining a failing project, the likelihood is that people are not feeling terribly motivated. There are as many ways to inspire morale as there are people. I will therefore not advise on specific strategies. Team building days have their place, but I

---

* You may also include a fourth bullet: sign here.

think there is a broader view to be taken. You might like to consider the following:

- Be a leader. A lack of morale often comes from a lack of leadership, so show some leadership. I said earlier in the chapter that you must speak to individuals and let them know that you are taking ownership of the project now. Let the team know that a page has been turned and help them to bury the demons of the past. Let the team know you are in charge now – not by a display of machismo, but by a quiet display of determination to get the job done. Remember, one of the best ways to lead is to support (and visibly show support for) your troops. To that end…
- Who needs additional support? It's possible that some people have been working all the hours God sends to keep the project on track. Who could do with some help? Or some time off? How can you make that happen? Even if you can't offer help directly, recognition often goes a long way. If someone is going over and above to keep things going, let them know that you know – and that you appreciate their efforts. Lack of recognition for your efforts is hugely demoralizing, but giving that recognition is easy and will be a welcome act of kindness.
- What are the things stopping people from doing their job? It is frustrating to come up against roadblocks when you are trying to get a job done. It is more frustrating when it is outside your control to remove them. Speak to the team and find out what are the roadblocks they face. Between you and your Sponsor, it's likely you have the ability and the authority to work on removing these impediments to people getting their job done.
- Morale applies up and down the chain of command. Poorly managed stakeholder expectations will also start to damage your project, so it isn't just the morale of your project team you need to consider. Does your Sponsor need a bit of support to feel positive about the project again? As with your team, let the Sponsor know that you are taking charge now and that a new page has been turned. Help the Sponsor to bury their demons too.
- Sympathize and empathize, but don't get dragged down. You need to stay positive. Your message needs to be that the project is recoverable and that you will put the changes in place to make that achievable. Some people on the project may have been working for some time

in a toxic environment. You need to sympathize with them. Some people may have been working beyond their contracted hours for months. You need to empathize with them. But don't get drawn into a whirlpool of negativity. Listen to them, but make sure that, at the appropriate time, you draw a line under the past and encourage the team to look forward.

EVERYTHING'S FINE UNTIL IT'S NOT (AND NOW IT'S NOT)

As noted in Chapter 7, when things are going well, people have a tendency to quietly drop governance, or other good habits that you rely on when the chips are down. Maybe they've stopped updating the plan, so we are now blissfully unaware that a major milestone will be missed in three weeks' time. Or maybe they stopped keeping their Sponsor updated, as there has been nothing to report for so long, but if they had kept it up, a couple of the issues now being experienced might at least have appeared as an "amber" heads-up in the last few reports.

Worse yet, maybe the project is in bad shape because *no* governance was ever established. In either case it is important to ensure that piece by piece your governance – the very set of mechanisms that are designed to protect projects from failure – is put into place. Establish what the cost baseline is (or should be if one has not been agreed). Pin down the key milestones and aim to get a quick understanding of how the project is performing against them. Where is the signed-off scope – how much of it has been delivered already and how far have we deviated from delivering it? Get a Steering Group and get them briefed that they will need to be on high alert to help you as you turn this project around. It doesn't need to be dramatic though – just get some governance in place and start using it.

LEAVE THE FIREFIGHTING TO THE FIREFIGHTERS

This is a subset of "you are not the expert." If a project is failing, that means it is failing to meet its obligations by delivering the objectives within the expected time, cost, and quality constraints. That is where your focus must be. You need to, with your team, figure out what needs to be done to get the project back on track. Then, as project manager, your job is to *manage* that activity. There may be certain tasks that it makes sense for you to do, so do them. But your primary responsibility is to manage the project the same as any other. If a failing project can be compared to a fire, the role of the project manager is to coordinate everyone else's activity – not to pick up a hose. Leave the firefighting to the firefighters. Your job is to take a high-level view of the actions that need to be taken – and then assign them to others.

WHO'S DOING WHAT?

Are the right people involved? And do they know what they're supposed to be doing? Go back to roles and responsibilities – consider who you need on the project and whether there is somebody who is a good fit for each role. You will end up with three activities you need to undertake:

- Where there is a person acting in a role: confirm their role back to them. Ensure they are happy in that role and aware of what they are expected to deliver.
- Where there isn't a suitable person for a given role: plug the gaps. You've identified that your project team is missing a person – this is progress. Now you need to come up with a plan to ensure that the role gets filled.
- Where there is a person with no clear role: make a decision on how best to use them, but recognize that they are not performing a project role. Projects, especially high-profile, exciting-looking ones, have a habit of attracting hangers-on. It is not unusual to inherit a project team only to realize that one or more people do not have a defined role to carry out and are adding no (or minimal) value to the project. Sometimes it is appropriate to keep them involved. Maybe they're a senior stakeholder, a useful sounding board, or a thoughtful ally. Sometimes though, the best thing you can do is have the difficult conversation and suggest they move on from the project.*

---

* It might be difficult, but it doesn't have to be unpleasant. In most such situations, the intentions are good – the person concerned just isn't required. They may even agree that they are not needed, but felt compelled to stay involved as they thought it was expected of them. In any case, if there is a considerate way to get the message across, it will serve you well to find it.

JFDI* PROJECTS

There's an old story about an actor who was struggling to understand why his character behaved a certain way in one of his scenes. He went to the director and asked the classic question.

> "This makes no sense. What's my motivation?"
> The director paused for a long moment before giving his answer.
> "Your paycheck."

It is not unusual for the Sponsor to be completely uninterested in the niceties of project management. So while you are desperately trying to draw up a table of benefits, or inspire a rag-tag, demotivated team to greatness, the Sponsor cares only about the stated outcome – irrespective of the means, the casualties, or whether there is any value in it.

There can be a number of reasons for this and it often helps to consider why the Sponsor considers it is so imperative that something is done, yet no-one seems able to give you a reason for doing it. The answer is usually political – for example, the Sponsor has promised *their* manager that something will be done and now, for reasons of saving face, The Thing Must Be Done, regardless of whether it will help matters – it may even be counterproductive. A commitment has been made and now you have been left to deliver it. What should you do?

Believe it or not, this is just a regular project, but one where scope has been prioritized – get me *this*. It is normal for these projects also to have a strong emphasis on schedule – get me this *now*. The counter is therefore to agree that it absolutely can be done, but the cost will be high because you need a team of 30 people instantly mobilized. This will not come cheap but if a person really JUST WANTS THIS DONE, then the sensible project management response is to sit in a room and brainstorm. No idea is too silly – everyone thinking outside the box. If all barriers were taken away, how do you get the job done? Then estimate the cost of that plan and (possibly while stating that you recognize it is too expensive) take it to your Sponsor. If they *really* want it done, you might find yourself surprised

---

* The politest interpretation of this acronym is "Just Focus and Do It." In my experience, the "F" usually stands for something a bit more robust.

(amazed, frankly) as they sign it off and you need to turn your wacky plan into action. This technique is intended to do two things though:

- Show the Sponsor that you are not dismissing it out of hand or saying it can't be done – only that it won't be easy.
- It creates a deliberately exaggerated starting position for you to begin negotiations with your Sponsor. If they accept that the project can indeed be done tomorrow, but are not prepared to part with the million dollar price tag, you can start to wind the position back. What if we delivered in two weeks for half a million? What if you just did this bit now and got the rest later for a quarter of a million? And so on.

Begin the negotiation and hopefully you will be able to work back to a point where the Sponsor gets the element that they really want, in a timescale that is acceptable to them, for a palatable cost. At the same time, you have a more clearly defined objective and have created the space necessary for you to realistically deliver it.

It is also worth pointing out that if the sponsoring party is not prepared to engage in normal project practice, then nor can the project be judged according to normal project success criteria. Get early agreement that the project is "exceptional" and (if necessary) that you are working on a "best endeavors" basis. That is, you will do your best to apply project practice, but cannot be held responsible when best practice is sacrificed for JFD-ing it. Responsibility for failure, in that instance, lies with those instructing you to JFDI at the expense of doing it properly.

MANAGING A PROJECT THAT CANNOT NOW SUCCEED

I sincerely hope that, in most cases, you will be able to find a way to turn an ailing project around. There will always be projects, however, that some poor project manager is handed only to find it is too far gone to ever achieve its objectives (assuming they were known in the first place – which they probably weren't). Some projects, like zombies in the movies, have a habit of staggering on long after the point at which, by rights, they should have died a quiet death.

My advice is simply this: once you have satisfied yourself that the project is really – *really* – past the point of saving, do **not** be the person who keeps it going any longer. You are not adding value (in fact you are costing more money) by trying to breathe life into it. It can often be a difficult, or politically unwelcome message* to say that the project must be stopped to prevent any further money and time being wasted. But from a purely practical point of view, the sooner zombie projects are stopped, the sooner all those involved can invest their time more fruitfully, and those funding the project can cut their losses and put their money to better use.

If delivering that message is simply not possible (or if the message is rejected) then you must move into damage limitation mode. I have found that the best and simplest way to do this is to review the scope with a view to reducing it as much as possible. If the project **must** be kept alive, ensure that it is redesigned to deliver those things that it **can** deliver and nothing more.

LESSONS LEARNED

The final thing to consider in this book is – perhaps appropriately – "what have we learned?"

In this book and in every project you undertake, the cheapest education you can have is to learn from your mistakes. Good project managers (and sensible people in general) recognize that there is value in reviewing a piece of work from a distance and understanding what you would do differently next time. This is an often-overlooked, or rushed, or poorly delivered part of the project management process but it is worth a few minutes of our time here, because if you don't stop and take stock – how on earth do you learn?

Most project management courses will tell you to undertake a lessons learned session at the end of your project as a piece of cheap learning. While this is not, of itself, a bad suggestion, I feel it misses the point. I have lost count of the number of lessons learned sessions I have been in where the point seemed to be merely to record the project's failings. And I

------

* I recognize it may even be a politically impossible message – in which case, all you can do is put as many project safeguards in place as possible, while accepting the likely inevitable conclusion.

ask you – honestly – what good is that? Whilst it might seem cathartic to get in a room and beat ourselves with birch twigs, little benefit is actually derived from sitting around and agreeing what we did wrong.

Similarly, I have been asked to contribute to many a lessons learned log. These are documents that are intended (quite honorably) as a source of knowledge for any projects that follow. I will make a controversial suggestion now: they are a complete waste of time.

If something went wrong on your project, there is absolutely no benefit **whatsoever** in just writing it down in the hope that some other hapless project manager reads it and decides it might just possibly apply to their project. What, then, should you do?

You go back to the process. If something goes wrong it is insufficient to say "avoid doing *this*" – you must change the process to ensure that doing *that* is impossible. This is the approach taken by the worlds of aviation and spaceflight, and from which I take my lead with regards to lessons learned. If a plane crashes, or a space shuttle explodes there is a lengthy investigation, followed – importantly – by procedural changes. It does not do just to write down "This went wrong." But you will find that this is the level of sophistication of most lessons learned logs. The very idea of a lessons learned log is foolish to me. If you have a log, you are not learning the lesson. Make a change to your process and you don't need to "log" anything.

THE EVERYDAY PROJECT MANAGER SHOULD...

- Always go back to first principles – what are the objectives? What are the expectations in terms of time, cost, and quality? Can we define these without completely stopping?
- Speak to as many people as you can to get a rounded view of what's happened so far.
- Leave the firefighting to the firefighters.
- Avoid keeping a dead project alive for the sake of appearances.
- Learn lessons – by making changes.

Appendices

In Summary: Delivering a Project in Three Pages

THE EVERYDAY PROJECT MANAGER SHOULD...

The following combines all my top tips from each chapter (those summaries at the end). However, by collating them here in one place, you can walk through them all at once, to use them as a health-check on your project. Use these as a refresher for what you need to be doing at each stage of your project and check that you have the basics covered. Enjoy!

PROJECT START-UP

- Understand the over-arching vision (if applicable).
- Have clearly defined benefits, with associated measures that are agreed with – and owned by – the Project Sponsor.
- Have a short list of up to five objectives (no more), with defined success criteria, that are clearly linked to the project benefits, also agreed with the Project Sponsor.
- Remember: if you are not delivering the objectives, you are not delivering the project.
- Understand the competing challenges of time, cost, and quality.
- Agree up-front which of them will have the upper hand in decision-making.
- Use the levers available to enable the project to adapt to changes and challenges ("Go faster!")
- Keep an eye on changes to ensure they are kept to a minimum.
- Start with a scope outline and then build a set of clearly defined requirements to ensure everyone is clear on how the end-product should feel.

- Wherever possible, satisfy yourself that each requirement links back to one of the project objectives.
- Assign a priority to each requirement – you could score them from 1 to 5 in terms of importance, or use a system like MoSCoW ratings.
- Be vigilant for scope creep.
- Ensure everyone on the team has a role and knows their responsibilities.
- Be conscious of the difference between a team member and a stakeholder. Make sure you're aware of who isn't on the team and manage them appropriately.
- Have a RACI – at least in your head.

DESIGN AND PLANNING

- Plan tasks and sequences forwards from a start date, not backwards from an end date (wherever possible).
- Plan to the right level of detail – don't get lost in the weeds.
- Ensure every task has an agreed owner.
- Use planning horizons (it's better to be broadly right than precisely wrong).
- Identify your pitons and firebreaks – ensure you have break-points that you can fall back to.
- Baseline your plan and then update it regularly. Ensure it adapts to changes as they occur, but do not allow tasks to slip unchallenged.
- Establish a baseline budget and track it in a cost plan.
- Have a simple cost plan that makes sense to you – and update it regularly.
- Ensure your cost plan is aligned to your schedule.
- Make allowances within your cost plan for contingency and risk, but sacrifice each as you go.
- Allow change to happen, but only under control.
- Set baselines and defend them.
- Use a regular report to sum up your progress and check you are staying on top of all the different aspects of your project.
- Know your escalation path and don't be afraid to use it.

BUILD AND EXECUTE

- Listen to what your team is telling you and watch how they interact with each other (and with you) in order to get the best from them.
- Use your own voice.
- Create and act according to your own authority. Do not invoke the authority of others.
- Be on the lookout for misleading, or downright deceitful, behaviors.
- Ensure the success of your project by supporting your team and ensuring each individual is successful in their role.
- Spend time considering all the things that might endanger the delivery of your objectives.
- Score your risks according to impact and probability, then focus on mitigating each.
- Be mindful of things that look and sound like risks, but are not for your project to fix.
- Budget for risks so that you do not have to find additional funds when a reasonably foreseeable event occurs.
- Implement your mitigations – but don't waste time trying to mitigate every last risk.

PROJECT CLOSURE AND LESSONS LEARNED

- Always go back to first principles – what are the objectives? What are the expectations in terms of time, cost, and quality? Can we define these without completely stopping?
- Speak to as many people as you can to get a rounded view of what's happened so far.
- Leave the firefighting to the firefighters.
- Avoid keeping a dead project alive for the sake of appearances.
- Learn lessons – by making changes.

Key Information for Every (Everyday) Project

The following plan can be used as means of capturing all the key project information.* It summarizes the project and provides the information in a way that is accessible to anyone involved (Table A.1).

TABLE A.1

Key project information

PROJECT NAME:			
Project manager:		**Project sponsor:**	
Benefit(s)	We want to achieve the following:		
	Benefit 1:		
	Benefit 2:		
	Benefit 3:		
Objectives	Objective 1:		
	Objective 2:		
	Objective 3:		
	Objective 4:		
	Objective 5:		
	Baselines vs progress		
Key dates	**Milestone description**	**Baseline date**	**Current forecast date**
	Milestone 1	Date 1	Forecast 1
	Milestone 2	Date 2	Forecast 2
	Milestone 3	Date 3	Forecast 3
	Milestone 4	Date 4	Forecast 4
	Milestone 5	Date 5	Forecast 5
	Milestone 6	Date 6	Forecast 6
	Milestone 7	Date 7	Forecast 7

(Continued)

---

* A downloadable version is available on the website everydaypm.co.uk/templates.

TABLE A.1 (CONTINUED)

	Milestone 8	Date 8	Forecast 8
	Milestone 9	Date 9	Forecast 9
	Milestone 10	Date 10	Forecast 10
Total budget	**Baseline budget**	**Spend to date**	**Anticipated final cost**
	Budget	Spend	AFC
Other project information: *(optional – add your own, specific to your project)*	The full list of requirements can be found here: *<Requirements location>*		
	The project folder can be found here: *<Folder location>*		
	The project manager can be contacted on 01234 567 890 or by emailing project.manager@mycompany.com.		

Index

Printed in Great Britain
by Amazon

12198919R00142